PARISIAN
CHARM SCHOOL

French Secrets for Cultivating
Love, Joy, and That Certain
je ne sais quoi

JAMIE CAT CALLAN

A TarcherPerigee Book

tarcherperigee

An imprint of Penguin Random House LLC
375 Hudson Street
New York, New York 10014

Illustrations © Donna Mehalko

TarcherPerigee with tp colophon is a registered trademark of
Penguin Random House LLC.

Most TarcherPerigee books are available at special quantity discounts for bulk
purchase for sales promotions, premiums, fund-raising, and educational needs.
Special books or book excerpts also can be created to fit specific needs.
For details, write: SpecialMarkets@penguinrandomhouse.com.

Library of Congress Cataloging-in-Publication Data
Names: Callan, Jamie Cat, author.
Title: Parisian charm school : French secrets for cultivating love, joy,
and that certain je ne sais quoi / Jamie Cat Callan.
Description: New York : TarcherPerigee, [2018] |
Includes bibliographical references and index. |
Identifiers: LCCN 2017044382 (print) | LCCN 2017051138 (ebook) |
ISBN 9781524704797 (ebook) | ISBN 9780143130963 (hardback)
Subjects: LCSH: Women—France—Psychology. | Beauty, Personal. |
Charm. | Fashion. | French—Social life and customs. | Women—France—
Social life and customs. | BISAC: SELF-HELP / Personal Growth /
Happiness. | SELF-HELP / Personal Growth / Self-Esteem. |
FAMILY & RELATIONSHIPS / Love & Romance.
Classification: LCC HQ1206 (ebook) | LCC HQ1206 .C236 2018 (print) |
DDC 155.3/33—dc23
LC record available at https://lccn.loc.gov/2017044382

Printed in the United States of America
3   5   7   9   10   8   6   4   2

Book design by Sabrina Bowers

FOR SYLVIE

Contents

If I want to seduce a man, I won't show him I'm interested in him,

but I will show him I am an interesting woman!

You see the difference?

—EDITH DE BELLEVILLE, PARIS 2016

Présentation

IT'S A WEDNESDAY AFTERNOON IN LATE SEP-tember. It's my first French lesson with the mysterious Madame M. On this particular afternoon, for our very first meeting, I arrive at Madame M.'s home precisely at three o'clock. Okay, I actually arrive at seven minutes after three. I am still reeling from my drive to her cottage in the woods, the slow approach down the steep and narrow path lined with ancient pine trees that seem to whisper to me, demanding that I respect the quiet in the cool autumn air. I park my car behind an aging silver Camry. And then I stand at her door, feeling as if I am now in the realm of the fairies, swept into an enchantment, where there are heart-shaped stones collected by the steps and the door-knocker is shaped like a dragonfly. I am thinking about the song "Over the River and Through the Woods" when Madame M. opens her door. She is a *femme d'un certain age* to be sure, what that age might be, I honestly couldn't tell you. She wears her white-blond hair pulled up in an iconic French twist. She wears a cream-colored cardigan and an almost-but-not-quite-matching pencil skirt. She is wearing a delicate shade of pink/plum lip-stick and a plum-toned silk scarf that's artfully tied around her neck. She smiles at me, seemingly amused, and I can't help but think how she looks uncannily like my own French grandmother,

1

now long gone. But, honestly, it feels as if—here she is: my French grandmother, alive again, in front of me. And at this moment, I know without a doubt that a new story is about to begin.

I have come to Madame M. to become fluent in French. At this point, I do not yet know that I am about to become fluent in so much more than simply French. I am about to become fluent in the secrets of French women, the mystery of allurement, and the language of charm.

After greetings in French—*Bonjour, comment t'allez vous?*—she leads me into her home, past the radiant heat of the blazing fire in the fireplace, and around the table with wildflowers in little vases (I will learn later that she takes a walk every day in the woods and collects these flowers). She turns to me with intelligent eyes and tells me, *"La ponctualité est la politesse des rois."*

Madame M. waits for me to tease out what this means. She is patient as I reach back into the recesses of my mind to reconstruct the words from all the French classes and numerous visits to France to figure out that *La ponctualité est la politesse des rois* means "Punctuality is the politeness of kings."

After this, I will never be late again.

Okay, maybe a little late, but I will always make sure to call to let her know, and Madame M. will always say, in French, of course, that I shouldn't worry and to drive carefully.

Weeks go by and then months and then years. We read poems and stories about Paris in the fin de siècle and the life of French farmers in the country. We translate poetry from Verlaine and Voltaire. We talk about the philosophy of Montaigne. We discuss politics and the difference between the French and the Americans. Sometimes we forget that I'm supposed to be improving my French and we switch to English because what Madame M. wants to tell me is too important to be lost in translation.

And we talk about love. A lot. We talk about men. A lot. We talk about how a woman can garner the attention of a man she has just met, without the slightest hint that she might be dreaming of more. Madame M. tells me it's important to keep a man guessing, wondering. This is what keeps love alive and growing. We talk about French dinner parties and her occupied village during World War II. We talk about how she met an American GI and then came to America as a young woman to teach English at Wellesley College.

As time goes by, my French improves, but more than this, Madame M. teaches me about something much more important than my subjunctive verbs (regular and irregular)—she teaches me about the power of charm.

Yes, *charm*. This is what makes French women truly irresistible. This is what truly captivates the heart. Above all the secrets to French allure and how French women find and keep love, how French women earn the reputation for being mysterious and stylish, without a doubt, the cornerstone is charm. In fact, the highest compliment Madame M. will ever give you is *Trés charmant!* (very charming).

Many things have happened since I began my studies with Madame M. For one, I wrote three books on the topic of French women's secrets to love, joie de vivre, beauty, style, and *Ooh la la!* To research these books, I traveled to France many, many times, and stayed at the homes of many French women in the cities— Paris, of course, but also in the little villages in the country. In 2009 and again in 2016, I received artist fellowships from the Virginia Center for the Creative Arts to live for a time in the little village of Auvillar in the southwest of France. I've stayed with friends in Toulouse, Besançon, Lille, Dijon, and Gien, and I've discovered my French ancestors' homeland in Normandy. I've traveled all around France, by train and by car. And while many people are familiar with the delights of Paris and Provence, I have found that the true heart center of France and the French people can be found in the little undiscovered villages in the countryside, where, yes, sometimes, French women do get fat, and sometimes they do get sad and lose their sense of joie de vivre for a time, but they still live a life filled with charm.

And so, for the past ten years, I have made it my life's mission to study all things French. I've interviewed over a thousand French people (women *and* men). I've met with French teachers, artists, doctors, lawyers, administrators, pharmacists, dress designers, shopkeepers, hairdressers, estheticians, laborers, and beauty experts.

I'm proud to say I am good friends with Madame Cadolle, the director of the world's premiere haute couture lingerie company, Maison Cadolle, and the great-granddaughter of Herminie Cadolle, the woman who invented the modern-day bra in 1890. I count as my dear friends Elizabeth Bard (author of *Lunch in Paris* and *Picnic in Provence*); Kate Kemp-Griffin (author of *Paris Undressed*); Beatrice, who lives in Toulouse and who is a top appointee in the French health-care system; and Sylvie, a bohemian artist, filmmaker, and translator. She was my first French girlfriend, and I often slept on the couch in her charming Left Bank studio apartment, right off Boulevard Saint-Germain.

I've written about Sylvie in my previous books. Jessica Lee introduced me to her, and in turn, Sylvie is the one who organized the very first French Girl Party for *French Women Don't Sleep Alone*. Through her introductions and very generous friends, we learned the secrets to French women and love. Sylvie took Jessica and me through the winding streets of the Latin Quarter, across the Seine, past the booksellers, over to the Louvre and the Tuileries, to the Musée d'Orsay. We sat in countless cafés, climbed the steps at Sacré-Coeur, drank a lot of red wine, and talked-talked-talked, deconstructing the secrets of French women. Sylvie shared with Jessica and me her thoughts on how French women don't date, but have dinner parties.

Sylvie showed me where to shop on the Left Bank. She brought me to her number one top secret favorite Paris boutique. She challenged me when I made generalities about how all French women do this or that. I think this might be one of my favorite personality traits of the French woman: she likes to challenge you. She keeps you on your toes, and for someone like me—who likes to dance, both literally and intellectually—this is a great gift.

I am also so very grateful to Tania Fovart, a good French girlfriend who accompanied me on the trip of a lifetime. Together, we drove to the countryside in Normandy, where I made a pilgrimage to my ancestors' little village of Saint-Nicolas-d'Aliermont and visited the cathedral where

French charm has nothing to do with how much money you have, or how pretty you are.

my great-great-grandparents were married.

I have found that rediscovering my own heritage has given me a sense of what it really means to be French and what it means to possess charm. I learned that French charm has nothing to do with how much money you have, or how pretty you are, or popular you are, or well connected, or how many cute outfits you happen to own. It does have everything to do with making the most of what was given to you at birth, and even more important, what you do with life's challenges.

French women have explained to me that part of their heritage is to "put a flower on it." In fact, they seem to like to "put a flower" on everything. This means that even if your jacket is worn and slightly tattered—as many of the French women's jackets were after the war—you can still put a little flower in your lapel. In fact, to wear a flower in this instance is an act of courage and a show of defiance.

Perhaps this is why a French woman believes it's important to always dress nicely, even if she is staying at home, but especially when she leaves the home. French women know that when a woman is well groomed and wearing something thoughtful and charming she is a delight to all those around her. And most important, she delights herself. When she is out and about, her courage and charm enliven the world and encourage *le regard* (the look). And she also shares in the universal message of dignity, hope, and joy, not to mention the delights of being noticed by men.

Now, this attention might seem alarming to us, but the truth is, French women are also reserved, careful, and considered when it comes to their clothing and style choices, and especially when it comes to their romantic relationships.

You might find the idea of charm to be a bit dated and a little old-fashioned. Perhaps it reminds you of the classes your grandmothers talked about, created in an effort to help a gal catch a husband. Or maybe it's something we talk about in our Jane

Austen book club or something we saw on a rerun of *Downton Abbey*? I wonder why we let go of the notion of charm and replaced it with the manners and mores of reality television, where charm has been shouted down by the loudest, the most shocking, the attention-grabbing women and men.

It's true that when it comes to our private love lives, we are living in a postmodern, just-too-cool, technologically fueled anti-romantic time where the idea of charm is now a cyber-wink on OkCupid or a swipe on Tinder and a provocative text message. Women are finding it difficult to simply meet a man face-to-face, let alone find the opportunity to talk and laugh and walk and take the slow, scenic route to love. And while cyber-dating seems like a "necessary evil," it can also cause much loneliness both on- and off-line.

Many women, and men, too, have given up on the idea of spontaneity, let alone the miracle of love at first sight—you know, that feeling that you have known that particular man in another life, perhaps. (My French teacher, Madame M., taught me that the French call this phenomenon *coupe de foudre,* or "a strike of lightning.")

Established couples sometimes find themselves trapped and perhaps even isolated by their own vows of commitment. And while they may still be completely in love, they sometimes feel captive within the confines of their own marriage. This is because many American couples have "collapsed" into a kind of passionless friendship and their partnership has settled into a predictable and overly safe routine.

If you're divorced or widowed and searching for a companion, well, then you quickly discover that while you were out of the American "dating scene," the world of love took a decidedly *uncharming* direction. Yes, we'd like to find love, passion, and companionship, but perhaps we're old enough to know that people are not always forthcoming and honest and it's best to be cautious and take our time before we engage our heart in a new liaison. And the loudest voices cry out, *Why wait?!* Everything is moving so fast, and if we want sex, well, it shouldn't be so difficult to find a willing co-conspirator. Certainly, there's an app for that. But, in the end, is this fulfilling, especially if we're looking for more than just a hookup, and we're really looking for a relationship, something beautiful and fulfilling and charming?

Charm can't survive in a world where love has become a transaction, ordered up on a smartphone, using algorithms that thrive on mobility, geographical connectivity, ease of delivery, and a predictable pattern. And who wants to be predictable, anyway?

Real romance takes time. Real romance requires patience, attention, and knowledge of who you are in this lifetime. And even if we find love online, it's important to note that charm can't be Googled. It must be cultivated. This takes time and patience and intelligence.

> *Charm can't be Googled. It must be cultivated.*

Yes, *intelligence.*

Let's take a cue from our French sisters and begin our search for romance by first creating a full life for ourselves, even if we are alone or brokenhearted or just feeling as if our days of love are all over.

Begin your journey of transformation by embracing the fine art of conversation, good manners, partner dancing, and dinner parties. Let's develop our sense of art and nature, self-love and self-care, and most important, a life of the mind. Even if you think you know all about these things, I suggest you look again at these time-proven techniques as a refresher course in how to be captivating.

Think of this book as your course syllabus. Each chapter is a new class, where you will learn how French women create a life where they feel confident and beautiful and strong and smart. At the end of each chapter, you'll find a *Parisian Charm School Lesson.* These will help you bring Parisian charm into your own life. You'll also get homework assignments (*pratiques*) and tips on how to develop your own individual charm.

One last word—be patient. Be gentle with yourself and confident that once you've finished your course studies and you've "graduated" from *Parisian Charm School,* you won't need to chase after love, because love will find you.

CHAPTER ONE

La Rentrée

(Back to School)

The only real elegance is in the mind;
if you've got that, the rest really comes from it.
—DIANA VREELAND

IT IS SEPTEMBER IN PARIS, AND WE ARE IN
the middle of *La Rentrée*. This is the time of year we might
describe as "back to school," but in France, the season has a bigger narrative because it's when most French people come back
from their six-week holiday, tanned, rested, and ready to begin
anew. It also signals big events around Paris, including Fashion
Week, the Salon du Vintage, Fête des Jardins, and Paris Design
Week. There's a lot of excitement over the new museum exhib-
its, concerts, ballet, and all the cultural happenings the City of
Light has to offer her devoted citizens. It's also the time of year
when France's top writers see their creations filling the bookstore
shelves.

I am here in Paris in search of a deeper understanding to the meaning of Parisian charm. After months and months of preparatory e-mails and phone calls, I have created a kind of course syllabus for myself—a semester's worth of research, reading, and conversation—my own do-it-yourself charm school.

And so, I arrive on this sunny day for my first meeting at Café de Flore on Boulevard Saint-Germain and I immediately see Edith de Belleville. You can't miss her. She stands in front of the café, looking very pretty, wearing her signature ensemble—a kerchief in her hair, a dress with a pattern of tiny red and white polka dots, red bangles to match, high heels, and a string of beads in the style of Coco Chanel. Edith and I give a *bisou* (a kiss) on each cheek and agree that the day is glorious and, ah, isn't Paris simply the most wonderful city in the world?

Edith hosts the rather famous *Edith's Paris*, tours specializing in literary Paris, as well as the great Parisian women in history. Her tours are informed by her insatiable interest in French social and literary history. She was educated at the Sorbonne and she's incredibly well-read. Edith was married to a Canadian, and while she has visited Toronto, she did not want to live in Canada because, as she tells it, *"It is too cold and impossible to wear high-heel shoes in the snow!"*

I realize that this is a French woman's particular gift—to be articulate and well traveled, but to take the conversation and effortlessly throw in a silly aside that makes you laugh and completely disarms you. And then, once disarmed, Edith will switch gears and give you a little lecture on the importance of Stendhal, the *Chambre Bleue,* and the great literary salons of seventeenth-century Paris life. She has a talent for presenting all this French social and literary history in a theatrical, slightly gossipy, and very funny style. Truly, after just a short time with Edith, you feel as if it's 1925 and you're hanging out at Harry's Bar at the Ritz with Hemingway and Fitzgerald, and look—in walks the barefoot artist's model, Kiki de Montparnasse. You can practically taste the sting of the dry whiskey and smell a cloud of French perfume.

And so Edith takes my arm and pulls me past the tourists and the couples sitting at the outdoor tables drinking their *café crème* or their espressos and watching the theater of life passing by on the sidewalk. Edith tells me that we will not sit outside, but inside the café, upstairs. This is where the true Parisians sit, she explains. This is where we can really talk.

I MET EDITH YEARS AGO during a book event at the American Library in Paris, where I was speaking with the author Harriet Welty Rochefort, author of *Joie de Vivre*. Edith was in the audience and she stood up during the question-and-answer period and pronounced—enthusiastically, and rather provocatively—that this whole idea of the French woman is a myth. *"There is no such thing as this quintessential French woman!"*

And then, with her passionate protestations, she went on to show in word and deed that she was the absolute embodiment of the quintessential French woman, because she was a mix of the most delightful and frustrating inconsistencies and a complete dichotomy. She was dressed all in vintage, wearing a red blazer with a silk flower at the lapel, and a flirty skirt, but her ideas were quite modern. She was sweet and smiled more than French women are known to smile, but she was also incredibly argumentative. In one moment she complimented me and in the next moment, she challenged me. More than anything else, she was completely her own person, and that made her very, very French and, yes, the quintessential French woman.

It's because of this original encounter that I wanted to meet with her and ask her about this thing called charm and why French women seem to have so much of it.

I follow Edith into the café, past the huge mirrors and the art deco posters of Paris, up the circular stairs to the upper floor. *"Simone de Beauvoir wrote* The Second Sex *while at the Café de Flore,"* she says, a little breathless, quickly negotiating with the waiter to find us the perfect table. *"*The Second Sex *sold over one million copies in the US in 1949 and two hundred thousand copies in the first week in France."* She gives me a serious look with her big brown eyes as we sit down at the red leather banquette, facing the window overlooking the bustling boulevard below. *"So you see, it's good luck for writers."*

We order coffee. Edith is talking-talking-talking. It's hard to keep up with her. She jumps from how Colette discovered Audrey Hepburn to play *Gigi* on Broadway to how she adores Swedish men, then on to Stendhal and Bonaparte and something called "crystallization"—a condition to describe falling in love beyond all reason.

Edith has a Louise Brooks–style black bob with bangs, mercurial mannerisms, and, as mentioned before, big brown eyes. Oh, and red lipstick.

She is a true *Parisienne*, born and bred in Belleville—across the street from Edith Piaf's birthplace, she tells me. *"I come from a working-class part of Paris, but I got a great education."*

When I ask her about the secret to Parisian charm, she tells me it's very simple. *"Develop your intellect. Don't show a man*

you're interested in him. Show him you're an interesting person."
She goes on to explain how even a high school student will have
eight hours of philosophy each week, where they read the literature of Nietzsche, Kant, Rousseau, and Freud, among many others. *"The French are expected to form their own opinions and to
be able to discuss and disagree, but still maintain their charm,"* she
explains to me. Edith tells me how when she was a teenager,
she attended the François Truffaut film festival, and how these
iconic French films from the 1960s made a tremendous impact
on her life.

Edith opens her purse, takes out a book, and hands it to me.
"Here, you can have this," she tells me. *"I didn't care for it."* I take
the book and thank her. It's a well-worn English language copy
of Lucy Wadham's *The Secret Life of France.* For a book she
doesn't like, it certainly has been read. The pages are warped
and as I flip through, I notice water stains inside. I wonder if she
read the book in the bath?

As we are talking, Edith spots a couple at a nearby table.
Actually, they are not exactly a couple. I turn to see an older,
gray-haired gentleman and a slightly younger woman with long
blond hair. She leans in and holds a small recorder up rather
close to the man's lips. He is pontificating about something or
other. I assume it's important, because he gestures, patting his
hand on the café table for emphasis, and the woman nods in
rapt attention, a serious expression on her pretty face.

"That's Laure Adler," Edith tells me. *"She's a famous journal-
ist. She's always in here, doing interviews."*

I glance over at their table again, as discreetly as possible, and
Edith whispers in my ear, *"She's a feminist intellectual. She wrote
the book* The Women Who Read Are Dangerous.*"* And then

Edith gives me a meaningful look. *"Les femmes qui lisent sont dangereuses."*

We sip our café and Edith gives me the history of Saint-Germain-des-Prés and how it became *the* place for intellectuals and artists, even surpassing Montparnasse. Edith tells me she is learning Chinese. *"That's how I flirt,"* she says. And then she tells me a story about how she has an admirer and she's known this man for quite a long time, but the other day, they happened to be with some people from China and without a moment's hesitation, she began speaking Chinese to them. Well, the admirer was startled. He had no idea she could speak Chinese! *"That's how the French flirt,"* she explains. *"This little surprise would not be nearly as effective if I just boasted—hey, I know Chinese! No, it's the surprise that makes it fun."*

I must admit I am enamored over this kind of flirtation. Perhaps it's because I admire education and reading, but I think it's more than that. I think I like this form of flirtation because it's available to anyone—anyone who wants to take the time to develop her intellect.

> *"Read, read, read! Feed your spirit."*

Edith's parting words to me, as I leave her, are: *"Read, read, read! Feed your spirit."*

GIRLS WHO WEAR GLASSES

My mother once told me that when she was coming of age in the 1940s, there was an expression, *Men don't make passes at girls who wear glasses.*

To our ears today, this sounds terribly dated. After all, especially now, eyeglasses are certainly having their style moment,
and we have entered an era where Jenna Lyons, the former
creative director of J.Crew, rocks the thick black brainiac frames.
Lately, we've seen eyeglasses on the models on the catwalk and
the runways in Paris, Milan, New York, and London. The Acad-
emy Award–winning actress Lupita Nyong'o is famous for her
fabulous eyeglasses. They have their own Twitter page! Young
women are buying up prescription-less eyeglasses in an effort to
cultivate the intellectual look.

It seems as if we are searching for a way to be taken seriously,
to be appreciated for our depth and sensitivity. It's as if we are
saying, *Please listen to me—I'm smart. I'm serious. Look, I'm
wearing eyeglasses!*

As women, I believe we all want the world to realize we're
complicated, we're sensitive, and when you look at us, there
is more than meets the eye. We're not just a pretty face and
we're not shallow or easily accessible. At the very least,
if you want to seduce us, you'll have to create a con-
vincing reason for us to take off our eyeglasses.

On a deeper level, those thick-framed eyeglasses are symbolic of a woman who sees the
world clearly, but also wants to keep people at a
slight distance. The eyeglasses serve as a kind of
buffer, an object that is the modern version of the
paper hand fan, something she can hide behind, create a little mystery, and slow down any potential ad-
mirers. Both eyeglasses and a paper hand fan can be
used to conceal and can be used to reveal. Both are powerful

props. Eyeglasses create the illusion, and perhaps proclaim the reality, that a woman is smart, well-read, intellectual, and interesting.

READING IS SEXY

All this is lovely, but truthfully, it's a shortcut to what French women have always known.

We must educate ourselves and we must bring together that most irresistible combination of beauty and brains. We must read. Yes, I am actually suggesting that the very first introductory class in Parisian Charm School is this: read some books.

And afterward, you can pile a few of them on top of your head and practice your posture, but that lesson is for another day.

Parisian Charm School Lesson

Before you can even approach the idea of captivating a man's heart, you must first captivate your own. There are lots of ways to discover (or rediscover) your own spark. French women do this by cultivating an intellectual life. As simple as this sounds, begin your journey by reading.

But, don't simply stay at home and read. Rather, you must go out into the world. Begin by going to your local library and taking some books out on loan.

FRENCH WOMEN KNOW THAT READING IS VERY SEXY.

Books love fresh air. It's true. The experience of reading is transformed when you get lost in the imaginary story, and then look up to see your world with new eyes. The leaves on the trees look a little greener, the air is warmer, and the sky is bluer. Read in the park, at a café, in a bookstore, or if it's a rainy day, read at the library. You can read from a tablet, but I would like to make the case for carrying an old-fashioned hardcover book with you. In fact, carry a big book with an interesting cover.

Consider that this book is an *objet d'art*, an artifact. It's a tangible object and it's also a great conversation starter. In fact, an interesting-looking book is a wonderful way to let someone know you're intelligent and curious about the world.

Reading a good book is the beginning because it will help you decide what you love, whether it's stories from the past or stories with an imaginary vision of the future. Then again, you might find yourself reading about the cure for polio, or jazz in the 1950s. Perhaps your books will be filled with pictures, art from the Fauvist period. From this first exploration, you can focus on what moves you on a deeper level. Is it dance, tennis, stargazing, or the science of beekeeping? If it's art, then look at your local event listings and attend the latest exhibitions. Be sure to look for receptions and openings at small, local galleries. Look for interesting workshops and classes.

This interest in culture and community is one of the most important secrets to charm. You will more than likely meet someone at such an event, and even if you don't, you will have something interesting to talk about when you find yourself with that handsome man next to you at the Stravinsky concert.

The truth is, when you're engaged in something you love to do, you are more naturally attractive, and you're probably not even thinking about meeting a man, which makes it even easier to meet one. So yes, begin with what you feel passionate about, and what makes you happy.

Begin with what you feel passionate about.

It's also important to move out of your comfort zone. Be vulnerable and willing to learn something you're not necessarily very good at and would like to learn more about. We tend to live in a self-service, do-it-yourself culture, but if you do everything yourself, you lose out on the opportunity for making new friends. Throughout France, you'll find daily lessons in cooking and dancing, and even guided tours throughout historic neighborhoods, where you can hire (for very little money) a local Parisian to take you for a walk and practice speaking French. Just consider how much more fun this is compared to wandering around all by yourself, with your French/English phrase book and map of Paris.

The basic message here is—get out of the house, do things, have fun, and more important, read a book!

Parisian Charm School Pratique

This week, check your local listings and attend at least one event (but no more than three). I highly recommend lectures at your local library.

Bring an interesting-looking book with you and talk to at least three people. If you're shy, then just smile and listen. Be patient. This is just the beginning of your transformation.

And for extra credit, get yourself a pair of eyeglasses, with or without prescription lenses. Experiment with them. See how they make you feel. Have fun with this.

CHAPTER TWO

The French Art of Reimaging

Know, first, who you are,
and then adorn yourself accordingly.
—EPICTETUS

TONIGHT, I AM WITH MY FRIEND ALOÏS AT the terrace of Le Hibou, a restaurant off of l'Odéon where we are enjoying champagne cocktails, a fruity mix with a little paper umbrella for decoration. Aloïs is a personal stylist and the creator of one of my favorite blogs, *Dress Like a Parisian.* Aloïs is twenty-nine years old and today, I would say she's dressed on the rock-'n'-roll side: her hair is short with longish bangs and she's wearing skinny jeans and biker boots.

Aloïs has a master's degree in law and a fashion degree from La Mode. When I ask her about this idea I have about how our personal and family history influences our style, she tells me that even when people are poorly dressed, there is still "a trail" of who they are. *"If you really notice things, you can get a sense of it."*

On the topic of fashion and style, Aloïs gives me a brief history lesson.

"Women in the 1950s wore matching things—hats, shoes, bags, and scarves. In those days, there was no real 'youth' trend, and women went from being a kid to being a grown-up. In the sixties, fashion for young people appeared, and along with that, more freedom. People still match, but it's important to be more complicated, more creative."

I ask her about her clients and what sort of woman seeks her out for a consultation. Aloïs sips thoughtfully on her drink and then looks up at me. *"When women come to see me, they're really open to trying new things. It's a transformational story. A sixty-year-old French woman came to see me a couple of years ago. Honestly, it's not really part of the French culture to consult a stylist and spend money on something they should already know."*

I nod my head. I had never realized that there is a certain burden on the French woman by way of reputation. If she's supposed to know all the beauty and style secrets from just being French, then I guess it is difficult to ask for help. That's one thing, as an American, I am not shy about. So perhaps we are lucky in this regard.

Aloïs continues her story about the French client. *"At first, I thought she looked like a nice grandma. Cute. I listened to her and paid full attention. She wore mossy green, but other than that, no real color. She was size forty-two, but had always been a size thirty-six."*

(Just as an aside, a forty-two is a US twelve and a thirty-six is a US size six.)

Aloïs gestures to show me the woman's size. *"Her body is*

well balanced. Not fat at all. Then she tells me she was a thirty-six all her life, but had cancer and stopped working for two years and then she returned to work and she felt like an old woman. She feels she cannot be seductive to her husband again.

"I rented a private room at Bon Marché. When she arrived, she had on an outfit with small prints. There was a lot going on." She shakes her head in dismay. *"And nothing going on! I picked out some skinny jeans. She has a flat belly. It's very good. But she has a pear shape and says, I cannot wear skinny jeans! And I show her that they actually make her hips look small."*

Aloïs describes how in addition to picking out a pair of dark blue skinny jeans, she chose a pair of suede boots in a caramel color with a little heel, a very simple silky top in a cream color with a V neck, and a gold pendant necklace. *"It was a really minimal look. She looks at herself in the mirror and cries. She has pale blue eyes. Now she looks like she's in her fifties, modern, energetic."* Aloïs gives me a meaningful look and finishes her story with a note of triumph. *"I got her to try Stan Smith limited-edition sneakers—the most popular ones in black with white soles. With the skinny jeans and a coat—it's hip and minimalistic. She thanked me later and said, my sneakers were such a success at the office!"*

I ask Aloïs where all this interest in fashion and style came from. She tells me her mother had a major influence on her life and always bought her nice clothes, but not necessarily what the other little French girls were wearing at the time.

"Even though I was a baby when I outgrew things quickly, my mother still bought quality. I remember when I was six years old, I loved an old purple outfit with a T-shirt and a little skirt with

white fringe. I wore it with a matching cardigan. The other girls in my school were wearing teddy bear leggings, but my mom got me jeans with a shirt and suspenders. It was very boyish, and not girly. Because of my mother I never wore stupid teddy bears and flowers!"

The evening winds down and Aloïs talks a little about her love life. Surprisingly, she is on Tinder and has lots to say about the men she meets online. First of all, they go from online to real time very quickly. And second of all, she only meets with the men who are good writers, send clever messages, and have a sense of humor and intelligence.

It's dark now, and the Left Bank has come alive with Parisians and tourists out for the evening. Aloïs and I stand at the crosswalk of the Rue de Condé. The streets and the cafés and bistros are now crowded. She stops at the Vélib' rack and retrieves her bike while giving me a running stream of advice for my readers. *"It's important to recognize the value of the work of people who make fashion. Stop buying cheap stuff!"* And then she gives me a little smile. *"Okay, the occasional H&M is fine. But go for quality. Support the artisans and good workmanship!"*

I nod my head as she gets on her Vélib' bike and pulls on a pair of chic leather gloves. Next, she adjusts her shoulder bag. *"And if you don't have the money, then be creative. Mix vintage with new."* She is about to pedal onto the boulevard. *"Never be too feminine, too girly. Never be too complicated. Too obvious. Never look like you're trying. But you must try!"*

> ## WHEN IT COMES TO STYLE, TRY NOT TO LOOK AS IF YOU'RE TRYING TOO HARD. BUT STILL, TRY YOU MUST!

She looks at me with a pout. *"And no logos! Okay, the occasional logo is fine, just don't cover yourself in logos!"*

I want to tell her that I don't wear logos, and I feel the sudden desire to defend all my American compatriots who have ever worn a logo, but my Parisian friend is gone into the black of night.

THE HOLLYWOOD CONNECTION

I am still trying to process my evening with Aloïs the next day when I meet with Rhonda Richford. Rhonda is the American correspondent in Paris for *The Hollywood Reporter* and she's been happily living in Paris for several years now. We have met for lunch at Café le Buci and she's brought her foster dog, who sits politely at her feet by our outdoor table. Rhonda tells me she is obsessed with a hot pink Ted Baker coat. She shows me a photo of the coat in question on her iPhone. *"I have to have this,"* she proclaims. I must admit, it's beautiful, and I now want one, too.

And then, before the salads even arrive, I ask her about my conversation with Aloïs. *"How is it that French women have all this confidence about style? Where do they get it?"* And then, I add, *"And more important, how can we get that confidence?!"*

Rhonda is a stylish gal, and I can see that in the time I first met her a few years ago, when she had just arrived in Paris, she has been truly transformed. In fact, she seems more stylish and more confident, so obviously Paris has worked its magic on her. Today, she is wearing skinny jeans and her jet-black hair is pulled back into a flawless chignon.

"They have all that history," Rhonda tells me. *"They've been thinking about this for centuries. Plus, they're surrounded by all these beautiful old buildings and all that tradition. If we destroy our historical roots, our old buildings, the traditions, if we hide away the aged, we erase the past and we erase our own truth, our heritage. The French understand this."*

STILL, THIS IS A REALITY for many of us. We walk around our cities and towns—or often, drive quickly by—and we don't really see or appreciate our own history. Our old buildings have been torn down and replaced by new ones, or shopping centers or office parks, and somehow the metaphorical bread crumbs that should help us find our way back to our ancestral home have been nibbled away by ravenous birds. And even if things aren't as bad as this may sound, we are still at a disadvantage in terms of our sense of style.

What to do? Rhonda suggests we read about our own culture. *"Watch old movies,"* she insists. She is a Hollywood girl, after all. *"Study the past, but don't try to be French! Look at your own culture and personal history for style."*

I love this idea, because if each of us truly knows and understands where we come from and what our style origins might be, then there is no need for comparison, or competition or jealousy, because each of us can take our own unique path. That could mean wearing cowboy boots from Texas. It could mean your first boyfriend's white shirt. It could mean our grandmother's hats, redesigned for a modern look. Perhaps it's a Shetland sweater your cousin wore or a sari your college friend only wore for special occasions. Your style could be influenced by the '60s, when you were obsessed with the Carnaby Street and the London mod look. Perhaps your key to style comes from your father's suits and ties, or your older brother's grunge style.

Rhonda tells me that I need to look up Nancy Cunard, a British heiress who came to Paris in the 1920s. She's best known for her multitude of wrist bangles from Africa. Man Ray famously photographed her wearing them and she became known as the queen of the jazz age, and she was truly a muse to modernism.

She published literary anthologies and traveled to New York City, where she met many of the African-American writers of the Harlem Renaissance.

Nancy Cunard has influenced many fashionable women such as Iris Apfel, a style icon and one of the stars in the *Advanced Style* documentary, and the star of her own documentary, *Iris*. These days, many young fashionistas follow her, perhaps not even realizing that she is a fashion descendent of Nancy Cunard, and that Nancy Cunard's look can be traced back to Harlem, circa 1920, and before that, Africa.

Our style evolves out of a conversation we are constantly having through time and place and many generations. It's how we communicate through visual and sensory cues. Perhaps you can no longer ask your grandmother, but I think it's important to face the fact that by a certain age, you have stepped into the role of mentor, and it's your turn to inspire and to pick up the conversation. Start to be aware of the history you reference and how much you actually do influence the men and women and children and grandchildren around you. This is the stuff of life. When you wear that silver lamé dress or those John Lennon–inspired eyeglasses, you are giving others permission to be free to express their deepest selves. And this leads to a kind of quiet confidence that is irresistibly captivating. You become charming and beguiling simply through the unspoken language of dress, style, and personal history. You walk through the streets as a woman with a rich and mysterious past.

YOU'RE IN THE NAVY NOW

Later that week, while visiting Toulouse, still thinking about what Rhonda and Alïos said, I discovered an unlikely style inspiration—a French naval officer's jacket. I found it in a little vintage shop called Le Grenier d'Anäis, on Rue Peyrolières, not too far from the Place du Capital.

When I first walked into the store, I imagined that there

wasn't anything in the shop that I would want to buy. But as a longtime devotee to vintage, I know that's how vintage shopping tends to be. It's generally hit or miss. You find everything you've always wanted or you find nothing at all. I assumed this shop was going to be a miss. Still, I wandered around the main floor, looking through dresses from the '50s, '60s, and '70s, hats, pocketbooks, scarves. But no, there was nothing that caught my eye. And then I climbed up the stairs and circled around the balcony, and just as I was about to give up, I saw them: a row of genuine never-been-worn French Navy jackets. Those French Navy officers must not be all that big, because I found one that fit me perfectly. And I'm five foot two!

Okay, I understand—to you, this might sound not at all appealing. A French Navy jacket? You're puzzled. Ah, but to me, this jacket feels as if my entire childhood has been handed to me in blue gabardine, brass buttons, and gold ribbons. My father was a lieutenant commander in the navy. I have lots of photos of him wearing his officer's jacket. My mother and father met at a USO dance at Yale University in the middle of World War II while my father was in the V-12 officer-training program. When I was growing up, every Monday night my father put on his navy jacket with the brass buttons, shined his shoes, got his hat, and left to teach at the Naval Reserve.

So for me, this jacket is representative of my own personal history. This jacket makes me happy. I am honoring my family's past, and especially my father. Wearing it, I feel more fully myself, like I'm sending the world a sly message about who I am.

EVERYONE LOVES A GAL IN A UNIFORM

Later, back in Paris, I discover that my naval jacket is a regular man magnet! Everywhere I go, men stop me and ask about the jacket. French men are especially enamored and want to know what rank my jacket is. As it turns out, it's a commander's jacket. My dad was a lieutenant commander, but hey, close enough!

The point is, you might be surprised to discover where your style references come from. They may just be right in front of you, or in your old photos, or in a vintage shop. Pay attention to how a particular article of clothing makes you feel. If something brings you a moment of joy, makes you smile or laugh or even cry—well, pay attention to that. There's a personal message hidden in this emotion, just for you, *mon amie.*

> AT A CERTAIN AGE, YOU STEP INTO THE ROLE OF MENTOR. ENJOY THIS DELICIOUS PHASE OF LIFE.

Oh, and if your jacket or skirt or hat or shoes make men notice—pay attention to that, too!

The truth is, when it comes to finding our sense of authentic beauty, as Americans, we have an interesting challenge. We live in a country filled with a variety of cultures, religions, and experiences. Each region has its own personality and history. This is one of the most wonderful, inspiring, and delightful things about America. But, when it comes to focusing in on your special beauty, your unique look—it can be confusing. There is no one "American look." And so I believe that we would be much better served if we look at our own family and ancestors for inspiration. Begin the process of finding your unique look by poring over old family photographs. Talk to your parents, your grandparents. Consider not just what looks good on you, but what makes you feel happy and confident.

So, how do you answer the question, *Who am I?*

Actually, it's not as difficult as it sounds. The answer lies somewhere in your body. Your body is your own personal *terroir*. This is a word the French use in winemaking to describe all the factors that give a wine a particular character, such as the angle of the sun, the composition of the soil and temperature of the air, the nature of the climate. The truth is, you have your own personal *terroir,* as well. It's the place where you were born and includes your deepest memories and a million little things that you can't quite fathom, such as how the clouds looked on your fifth birthday or the aroma of your mother's tomato sauce on the stove. It's that feeling of running across the green grass on your way to go to school. It's the time you tried on your first pair of high heels. It's the night you won first place in the science fair. It's that moment when you tried on your mother's evening gown and her black patent-leather

> *Your body is your own personal* terroir.

high-heel shoes. It's that first kiss, standing by the water tower with a boy named Bill.

Parisian Charm School Lesson

Ask yourself, how does a certain dress make you feel?

How does a fabric make you feel? Do you shiver a little in silk? Do you feel wistful in crinoline? Do you feel at home in flannel? And what about the color violet? And dusty rose? Are you transported to a time in the past that you only visited in a dream or saw in an old photo? Trust your instincts. Even if you don't quite know where this feeling of familiarity and happiness comes from, trust what it is telling you.

This is your *terroir.*

French women will tell you that when you know who you are, you are able to become more yourself, and then you naturally and easily become more confident. When you know who you are, you are more "contained" because you are confident, and as a result, you become more mysterious.

And then, you become captivating. Charming. And you attract love and friendship into your life. It's that simple. And yes, that complicated.

Parisian Charm School Pratique

Talk to your family about their lives and your ancestors. What would you consider to be your "birthright"? That could be as simple as the realization that your family is musical or the green-flecked eyes that you've inherited from your grandmother.

Go through your wardrobe and separate out what makes you happy and what makes you not so happy. Look for common themes in your clothing choices. Even if you keep buying a certain kind of blouse and you still don't like them, ask yourself what is it about this style that fascinates you and keeps attracting you. There is information for you even as you are bringing those fashion mistakes to the Goodwill.

Take notes while you're doing this, because as you discover your personal style, these notes with help you find important references, refine your individual taste, and build a strong foundation for creating your own unique look.

Find an old family photograph and ask yourself what relative captivates you the most. This person may be long gone, but they may be your muse. If you don't have old family photographs, look at photographs of fashion icons, artists, writers, actors, scientists, and singers. Your style inspiration might come from unexpected places, such as a Rousseau painting of the jungle or an old matchbox illustration. And don't limit yourself to only women. Men and animals and even robots can inspire. You may find your spark from watching vintage *Star Wars* again and again.

Consider what you wear and how it might make people happy and want to talk and perhaps flirt with you.

Ask yourself if you have a beautiful piece of jewelry that reveals your family history. Wear it every day for at least a month and see if you get comments.

For extra credit, try creating an unexpected combination, such as styling your hair like Andy Warhol and wear an Isadora Duncan–inspired gown. Above all, be creative and have fun.

CHAPTER THREE

The Romance of Dance

You will always reveal what you feel in
your heart by what you do in your movement.
—MARTHA GRAHAM

IT'S REALLY HOT INSIDE LE CARREAU DU
Temple, despite the fact that the hall is so spacious and the ceiling soars to great heights. We're almost in October now, and of course there's no air-conditioning. We're in Paris, after all. I am generally grateful that the French don't go in for air-conditioning all that much, because I always seem to be a bit chilled. However, today, I long for that cold. Le Carreau du Temple is a fourteenth-century covered market in the 3rd arrondissement on the Right Bank. I am here at the Salon du Vintage, and the event is really crowded. Ah, so this is where all the Parisians go on a Sunday afternoon in autumn. I struggle to push my way through the crowds and maneuver my way past the endless booths. Along the way, I take note of varieties of clothing: 1920s flapper dresses, beautiful silk *chinoiserie*, hats, well-worn leather jackets, *crepe de*

chine dresses from the 1940s, and American jeans from the 1970s. Who knew our vintage Levi's were worth so much!

Elvis is playing on the loudspeaker, beseeching us not to step on his blue suede shoes—really, as if I ever would dare to step on his blue suede shoes! The French men and women surrounding me speak in loud, urgent voices, discussing the virtues of silk versus rayon and why this or that item is overpriced or underpriced or where's the mirror. I can't help but register the fact that, contrary to everything I've been told up until now, the French can really be loud! I suppose, it's a matter of what's worth shouting about and exactly what's the price for that '78 record of Cab Calloway singing "Minnie the Moocher."

Yes, in addition to clothing and accessories, the Salon du Vintage features records and housewares, furniture, cameras, watches, toys, and art. I try on a silk kimono, but it's too big, and I play with the idea of buying vintage eyeglass frames. But truthfully, I find the crowd and the noise to be a bit daunting, and so I gradually make my way to the exit. This is when I catch the soulful, yearning chords of a violin and concertina playing a 1930s tango melody. I am hypnotically drawn in, and follow the music until I discover the tango duo, Edith and Marcelle. Both Edith and Marcelle are dressed in a tuxedo, except that Marcelle, who has a very short boy-style haircut, wears her tuxedo with the back facing front. There is something so transgressive about this scene, and because of that, it's very compelling. Edith is very feminine and ladylike, while Marcelle is the quintessential gentleman, except he (or she) is wearing heels and red lipstick and plenty of mascara. Marcelle also has the most adorable dimples and looks a whole lot like the actress Natalie Portman.

And, oh, the dancing. Let's not forget the dancing. It's the tango and it's sensual and romantic and so very graceful and full of emotion. A crowd gathers around Edith and Marcelle as they glide from one end of the room to the other.

I decide to stay at the Salon du Vintage. I decide I must learn the tango. I decide that this is the reason I came to Le Carreau du Temple in the first place. It wasn't for the vintage clothes. It was for this moment. Something stirs within me, and I decide in that moment that when I return home, my husband and I will sign up for tango lessons. I decide that tango will save our lives and that tango will keep us young and keep our marriage bright and brilliant and full of romance and love and emotion and beauty as we enter our sixties and beyond.

During a break, I learn that Edith is actually Céline, a tango teacher and a theatrical coach. She tells me she believes that tango brings us to a deeper knowledge of ourselves and our relationship with others. Edith is the character she plays as a dancer and burlesque performer:

> "I'm a storyteller at heart. I focus on the narrative and the intention behind each gesture, ensuring that each moment works to drive the story forward and gradually reveals the underlying meaning."

OUR BODIES TELL THE STORIES AND SECRETS THAT ONLY OUR HEARTS AND SOULS TRULY KNOW.

Marcelle is Chanelle Dumet. She trained as a ballet dancer for twelve years, moved to Paris, began taking tango lessons with Céline, and then fell in love with both tango and her teacher.

Together they became the dancing duo Edith and Marcelle. They have a devoted following and they perform and teach all over the world.

When you dance, you are multilingual.

That's because dance is a universal language. When you dance, you are multilingual. You are French. You are American. You are Brazilian. You are Hungarian. You are everything.

THANK YOU, MR. PILATES

Yes, there was once a Mr. Pilates. Joseph Hubertus Pilates was born in Germany in 1883. According to his biography, Pilates was a sickly child, and while interning in England during World War I, he struggled to maintain his health and in order to get stronger, he created a system of exercises, which he dubbed "Controllogy." In 1926, Pilates immigrated to the United States and opened up a studio in New York City, where he taught his technique to dancers from the New York City Ballet, including George Balanchine.

MUSCLE MEMORY

Here I am, stretched out on my floor mat, in my local Pilates class. I reach out for my toes, and this is when I suddenly have a very strong body memory.

I know these exercises.

I know them on a very deep level.

And just as suddenly, I am transported back to my childhood home in Stamford, Connecticut. I am six years old and my mother is teaching a group of neighborhood children in our living room. There are eight of us. We are rehearsing for our spring recital, and so we stand on the stairs, heads up, shoulders back. We place one hand on the banister and the other extended out in a straight line. We slowly walk down one step, then stop, kick out our right legs, then our left legs, and then step down again, all in perfect synchronization.

For many years, I assumed my mother just made up all these little routines and exercises or that she was just recalling what she had learned in her own dance classes and from dancing in vaudeville shows in the late 1920s. She was a tap-dancing star as a child and played in clubs and theaters up and down the east coast. When I was a little girl, she often appeared in community theater or local revues.

But, back to my Pilates class. Here I am, after over fifty years, and I find myself in the same position as I was in my mother's little dance classes. I am doing the exact same stretches. I have a muscle memory. Before I even make the mental connection, my body senses the familiar movements. My body remembers. And after watching a film about Martha Graham, the mother of modern dance, I realize I grew up studying modern dance and Pilates. I just didn't know it.

My mother passed away twenty years ago, so I cannot ask her about all this. I wish I could.

I know this: dance belongs to anyone who moves. And we all

move, even if it's limited to a bit of chair yoga. Our bodies hold the music of the soul, and speak in a language that only the heart can read.

WHY BALLET MATTERS

Every French woman you speak to will tell you they studied ballet as a child. It's their foundation to good posture, walking, and communicating without speaking. This is the secret ingredient to their famous mystery and confidence. They might not all be dancers, but you can bet they all know dance.

Partner dancing is particularly important because, as we all know, dancing leads to romance. All my French friends can do something called "Le Rock," which is very much like 1950s swing dancing. It's nice to see that swing dancing is also very popular here in America, and I happen to know a number of women who have found romance on the dance floor, right in their own hometown.

FRANCE IS IN THE AIR

I always fly to Paris on Air France. After all, I'm going to France, and I like to get in the mood as soon as I board my plane. Also, I like to hear everyone speaking French, and, okay, the food is better, too.

Here's the best part of the Air France flight: the flight safety video. It's like nothing you'd see on an American flight. First of all, it features five very chic, very pretty girls, wearing red, white, and blue striped Breton shirts and white or red flared dance skirts that twirl and swish as they perform little pantomimes showing how very important it is to wear your safety belt because it will not only "elegantly highlight your waistline," but also keep you safe. I love the adorable dance performance the girls do to explain how, in the event of an evacuation and the lights going out, you will simply follow the illuminated light down the aisle. Oh, and if you need to find the location of your life jacket, put on your very fashionable nerdy black eyeglasses and read the instructions.

At the finale, the girls take a bow, smile, and wave to us and the theater's red curtain goes down. Honestly, it made me want to applaud right there in my little airplane seat, and I probably would if it weren't for the rather haughty-looking gentleman sitting next to me reading *Le Monde* and frowning slightly.

Here's what's truly remarkable about the Air France video—they've taken the serious and sober issues surrounding safety and what to do in the event of an emergency and created an adorable and very feminine little bit of theater. And, there is dance, of course, because after all, this is a French airline. There are also costumes, red lipstick, and an homage to fashion and style. The girls all wear ballerina flats—or as the French call them, "ballerinas." Oh, and the playacting is funny and flirty and incredibly charming.

DANCING AT NINETY

Something magical happened at my dad's ninetieth birthday party. This was a few years ago when my husband and I were still living on Cape Cod (or Cape du Cod, as I used to call it). My dad was turning ninety years old and we held a party for him where we had lots of guests and food and drinks and, of course, cake. I decided I would invite my Zumba Gold instructor, Kelly, to come and lead a few dances. Kelly and I planned a surprise dance for my dad because he had been a lieutenant commander in the navy during World War II. We chose the Bette Midler version of the famous Andrews Sisters song "Boogie-Woogie Bugle Boy" and through a lucky set of circumstances, another friend just happened to have two navy officer jackets—with the stripes and brass buttons, as well as two hats to go with the "gentleman and an officer" look. This was a few years before I found my authentic French navy jacket in Toulouse.

Kelly and I were a big hit and my dad loved the performance, but that's not what this story is about. It's about what happened *after* our little show. Kelly put on some country music and led us in a line dance, and then she played some Edith Piaf, and this is when the magic happened. Everyone—I mean everyone—got up and partner danced. My brother and sister-in-law, my friends, husbands and wives and boyfriends and girlfriends and friends and me and my husband, and my dad and his girlfriend, Beverly, all danced! As I swayed back and forth, my arms around my husband, who I like to refer to as Dr. Thompson, I glanced over at my dad and Beverly. They were holding each other close, gazing into each other's eyes, and I knew I was witness to a private and powerful moment, and love. True love.

Birthdays aren't always easy, and a ninetieth birthday can be especially poignant, even difficult. I'm sure Beverly was thinking about this when she held her love in her arms. I'm sure she was grateful for each and every moment they shared. I'm positive that she must have stopped for a moment to grasp the preciousness of this dance.

Then again, knowing Beverly, who is a true no-nonsense

Mainer, she'd probably tell me I was being ridiculous. But I know the truth: she was deeply moved, because she was dancing with my father.

That's what dancing does to you. It stops time, even as you are moving, and it connects you to all the dancers who have come before you and who will continue after you. Dance is the body connecting to the soul. It is laughter and joy, and serious and silly and soulful. Dance is the silent voice of generations communicating with you through music and rhythm and breath.

> *Dance is the body connecting to the soul.*

Okay, and it's great exercise, too.

HOW ZUMBA SAVED MY LIFE

If you know a little Zumba, you can dance all over the world. Seriously. I've danced Zumba in France, in Spain, and even on the little island of Malta. Zumba is a dance/exercise that was created by a Colombian dancer. The combinations include salsa, merengue, cha-cha, Middle Eastern, belly dancing, Greek, African, and even country-western. And that's just to mention a few, because Zumba is truly international.

At my new home in the Hudson River Valley, I now take Zumba classes with Amy at my local gym. She's told me that dance makes her more confident and happy and that this confidence makes a difference in all aspects of her life, including the bedroom. *Ooh la la!*

I also take Zumba Gold classes, for senior citizens. I'm not yet officially a "senior citizen," but I do love my Zumba Gold classes. I study with Anne-Marie, and she plays songs from my youth—lots of disco and rock 'n' roll. We've cooled down to Leonard Cohen's "Hallelujah" and Adele's "Hello." For a while, we ended classes with Tim McGraw's song "Humble and Kind." I love the simple country lyrics written by Lori Mckenna that advise us to "hold the door, say please, say thank you," and to "shut off the AC and roll the windows down." Maybe it's because I actually remember rolling down the car windows. Maybe it's because I really believe we should say please and thank you. Maybe it's because despite all my city sophistication and affection for Paris, I am a country girl at heart.

"THIS ISN'T TEATIME!"

So, here I am in a Zumba class in Toulouse with the very energetic and very funny Renata.

She is a slender, very attractive girl with a big smile, white teeth, and long auburn hair. Oh, and she's wearing a dance top that says NEW YORK BALLET.

Apparently, I've kept the class waiting while I ran out to get a drink of water. She asks me in English, what time do I think this is—teatime?! I answer back in French, *"Non, c'est le moment pour la danse!"* (No, it's time to dance!) I feel I can joke with Renata because this is my second hour with her, dancing. I began the afternoon with Zumba Gold, and now I am in the regular Zumba class and perhaps I'm feeling a bit giddy and overheated.

And now, she tells the class that she has a song for me, *the visitor from far away!* In a moment, I am dancing with a dozen other ladies to "America's Sweetheart" by Elle King. We are kicking up our heels and doing a faux cowboy step and the lyrics catch me by surprise. *"Well, they say I'm too loud for this town. . . . What do you want from me? I'm not America's sweetheart . . . but you love me anyway."*

I am breathless from this dance and this feeling that this French girl can see my American history in my movements and my expressions. I have the most exquisite feeling of discovering a part of myself that I never saw before until I came to this dance class in this foreign city.

Later, Renata tells me about her experience as a dancer and how as a child her parents danced during intermissions at the cinema in Toulouse. She danced with them at a young age, wearing her very first dance shoes, a pair of bright silk blue toe shoes with ribbons crisscrossing up her slender ankles.

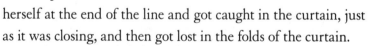

She was the smallest student in her dance class. She tells me this funny story of how they were doing a Scottish walk to end the performance. She found herself at the end of the line and got caught in the curtain, just as it was closing, and then got lost in the folds of the curtain.

> *"I ended up landing on the front of the stage, where everybody burst out laughing. It doesn't get better than that for a stage experience!"*

As we are leaving the *culturel centre* l'Espace Saint-Cyprien, Renata tells me how she's very interested in electronic and tribal music and culture. She has learned hip-hop, house, ragga, African, and even robotic dancing. She also practiced cabaret, salsa, tango, and music hall dancing. This was a revelation for the classically trained dancer. She tells me this:

> "It would seem that the charm was born the moment when my dance gestures started to express truths, or rather, accompanied with the gestural logic of my emotions, I was telling a story with my body."

Renata went on to get a master's degree in performing arts and cinema. She's also a burlesque artist. She tells me that she has created *feuille de séduction*, which is literally translated as "a seduction leafing" (the French term for a striptease), as an homage to Charlie Chaplin.

When I ask Renata about what dance means to her in terms of who she is and how she leads her life, she tells me she is guided by the principles of love and giving of oneself, and humility, onstage and in life. And finally, empathy and balance.

Your body can help you to be yourself more than you already are.

Before we say our goodbyes and leave for different metros, she gives me these words of wisdom:

> "Be yourself by listening to your senses in each gesture, every action, and its meaning. Just do that by itself without anything else. Your body has something to say to you. Listen to it. Your body can help you to be yourself more than you already are."

That is the power of dance. And honestly, I will never look at my Zumba classes as mere exercise ever again.

DANCING WITH THE STARS

The French have a long history and love of dancing. And even today, French boys and girls learn partner dance in school. Not only does this make young adults feel comfortable with the opposite sex, but also dancing makes them comfortable in their own skin, not to mention what it does for their posture and carriage. They have convinced me that it honestly does make you seem taller.

Last summer, when I was staying in Paris, I was delighted to find *Paris plages* (Paris beaches).

The city celebrates the hot summer weather by creating temporary beaches along the banks of the River Seine. Along with the sand and the lounge chairs, the mayor of Paris has added swimming pools suspended over the river, as well as concerts, and a pop-up mini version of the Louvre Museum. Of course, there's lots of dancing and dance lessons, especially as the sun goes down and the moon appears over the water, and the Eiffel Tower lights up and shimmers in the moonlight, under the brilliant stars.

Parisian Charm School Lesson

This brings me to why here in America we need to retrace our steps and find our way back to our roots (whether in Europe or Asia or South America or any country with a larger sense of history) and rediscover the old-fashioned love of dance. That dance might be the waltz or the tango or the foxtrot, but it is a dance that is about love, not competition.

Whether married or single, consider how you might bring dancing into your life on a regular basis. If you're in a relationship, put on some music and take your partner's hand. Dance in the kitchen. Even just a few minutes of impromptu dancing can mix the molecules and transform an ordinary moment into a romantic moment.

> ## DANCE EVERYWHERE—IN THE KITCHEN, AT THE OFFICE, WITH YOUR HUSBAND, WITH YOUR FRIENDS.

Find opportunities to dance in your very own community. Look up Argentine tango and you'll find a devoted community throughout the United States—in fact, throughout the world. Attend your local swing dance club. Many women in both France and America have told me how dancing is a great way to meet men.

Invite the muse of dance into your living room and into your life.

Consider hosting a party where you clear a dance floor for couples dancing. You don't have to get dressed in a navy officer costume, but you can put on a pair of dancing shoes and invite the muse of dance into your living room and into your life.

Parisian Charm School Pratique

Begin by dancing at home. Listen to your body and ask yourself what is it trying to tell you.

Listen to music and choose a style that resonates for you on a deep level.

Take a dance class. Begin with just one. See how it makes you feel.

Take your husband or boyfriend or best gal pal by the hand and sway back and forth. Don't even think about dancing quite yet. Simple close your eyes and listen to the sound of your breath and the beating of your heart.

CHAPTER FOUR

The Charming Benefits of Travel

Throw your dreams into space like a kite, and you do not know what it will bring back, a new life, a new friend, a new love, a new country.
—ANAÏS NIN

A FRENCH GIRL IN AMERICA

My dear Parisienne friend Sylvie first came to America in 1990 to work as a nanny for a French family in Connecticut. She fell in love with an American boy and lived in New York City for many years. Life took its twists and turns and she returned to live and work in Paris. She's the girl (okay, the woman) that Jessica and I stayed with when we came to Paris to host interview parties for my first book, *French Women Don't Sleep Alone*. Sylvie not only organized the events, but she took us on individualized tours around her beloved City of Light. And she took us to her secret shopping spots on the Left Bank and to the designer sales that only the Parisian cognoscenti know about and the cafés that are frequented by the locals and overlooked by the tourists. Sylvie was our guardian angel in Paris, so proud of her beautiful city and so generous in sharing Paris with us.

A few years ago, when my husband and I were still living on Cape Cod, before his retirement from Woods Hole Oceanographic Institution and before his new career as a gentleman farmer, Sylvie came to America and she and Jessica drove to the Cape to stay with us. Sylvie was in remission from breast cancer at the time, and she was quite thin, but not gaunt. In fact, her hair had grown back into a very cute pixie cut. She looked so pretty and happy in her French bikini, out in the water of Waquoit Bay, where my husband showed Sylvie and Jessica how to dig for clams with their feet, since we didn't have enough clam rakes to go around.

At lunchtime, we sat down at our dining room table by the galley kitchen and talked and laughed and ate in a delicious broth the steamed clams that we had just caught. And then, by special request from Sylvie, my husband made BLTs for us. This is because, before she arrived, we asked her what she would like and she told us how she remembered living on Sullivan Street in New York City and how she would go to a certain luncheonette on the Lower East Side and order a BLT. Apparently for this French girl, it was a revelation—bacon, lettuce, and tomato, along with Hellmann's mayonnaise, all in a sandwich!

My husband made the most amazing gourmet BLT for us that day. He fried really good bacon, and then he added fresh arugula and tomatoes from our garden on top of sliced crusty sourdough bread. He secured them with toothpicks to keep them from tumbling apart and brought the little sandwiches to the table with a flourish. We also had champagne, of course. This was, after all, a very special occasion.

Jessica and I oohed and aahed, and Sylvie agreed the sandwich was very good. But later, Sylvie confessed that she'd really wanted the true American BLT—on Wonder Bread with typical diner bacon and, get this, iceberg lettuce!

Truthfully, I could see her point, but still, in that moment, I saw the humble American BLT with new eyes—with French eyes. Sylvie made me see that my very own typical American life is charming. Yes, Wonder Bread and iceberg lettuce (seen from the vantage point of a visiting French girl) can be charming!

THE REINVENTION TOUR

Here's my favorite part about travel—it gives me permission to reinvent myself. But more than this, traveling gives me back my childhood. No, I didn't actually travel a lot as a child, except for those car trips from Connecticut to Key West when my dad was stationed at the Naval Reserve. Travel returns me to a kind of innocence—to those days in the early 1960s when I sat in the back of the 1954 Ford station wagon, staring out the window as we drove down US Route 1 through the small towns in the south. This was before the interstate highway now known as I-95 was carved into the north-south corridor, before there were thousands of channels on cable, before the Internet. This was during the days when there were four (or if you were lucky, five) television stations and no remote control. I'm not saying I'm nostalgic for these limitations, but I *am* nostalgic for that feeling of wonderment, when all of my senses were fully engaged in the struggle to comprehend the world and the people around me, and perhaps more important, to bear witness.

This is what travel brings to me.

When I am in France, I experience a kind of reawakening. My eyes, ears, sense of smell, taste, touch—and most of all my heart—are fully engaged in the challenge of understanding the mysteries before me. Why do the French dine all at the same time, in perfect order, as if someone made an announcement that it's time for lunch, and yet, they can't seem to queue up properly? I wonder how the French manage to hang on to the idea of *terroir* and the importance of festivals, celebrating everything from spring cleaning (the *vide grenier*) to the prune harvest in the southwest.

For me, the most delicious part of travel is the permission it grants me to be a child again and ask a whole lot of questions that might seem a little impertinent if I asked them in my own country. Why did you paint your walls bright yellow? When did you decide that your grandfather's *casquette* (workman's hat) would be your signature look? How do you organize your lingerie?

Highly impertinent!

Ah, but I am just an American lady and I want to know these things and somehow, for me, the foreigner, it's always okay. The Parisians and the people from all over France have opened their arms to me. And I do believe this is because I am sincerely interested and I am still that little girl staring out the window from the back of that Ford station wagon.

HOW TRAVEL CAN CHANGE YOUR DESTINY

Here I am at the home of Pierre and Frédérique, or as she likes this American to call her, "Freddie." I have taken the metro to Nation and walked to their home, entered the code, and taken the tiny gated elevator up to the fourth floor. Freddie greets me at the door and ushers me into their apartment, where light streams into the spacious room. We say our *bonjours* and give our *bisous* (kiss on each cheek) and I turn around to face the living room and I find myself falling under a kind of enchantment. Freddie and Pierre's home is filled with exotic mementos as a kind of homage to their adventures—a visual map tracing their travels around the world.

Their home feels like a Cabinet of Wonders. I walk around and notice all sorts of exotic icons and sculptures from Africa, Cuba, Colombia, southeast Asia, Chile, Bolivia, Peru, Ecuador, Nicaragua, and Honduras. When I ask about an ancient wooden table, Pierre explains that it's from Indonesia, and that another carved wooden cabinet is from nineteenth-century China. Freddie adds that they visited the Sumatra island in Indonesia.

"But Tanzania is truly my secret garden," she whispers to me as she gathers her yoga bag. I should explain that the French talk about their "secret garden" as a metaphorical place where you find your spiritual sustenance. It can be a literal garden at your home, or it could be taking violin lessons, or cooking or practicing yoga or even travel.

THE SECRET GARDEN IS A METAPHOR FOR A PLACE THAT NURTURES YOUR BODY, MIND, AND SPIRIT. IT CAN BE ANY PLACE YOU CHOOSE.

HOW FREDDIE FOUND PARADISE

A few days later, I meet Freddie at the café Le Fumoir, just around the corner from the Louvre. Freddie is wearing black pants and a hot pink jacquard top with a little bit of blue and red running through it. Freddie looks a lot like the French actress Audrey Tautou. She has light brown hair and big brown eyes and a kind of curiosity and sincerity that is completely disarming. And charming.

Le Fumoir is bustling with the Friday-night crowd.

We order the evening's special—monkfish with fingerling potatoes and *haricots verts* (green beans). We order a bottle of Orezza, a sparkling water from Corsica. She tells me it's very special, with delicate bubbles. Apparently, Perrier has not-so-delicate bubbles, and therefore is not as nice. *Who knew?*

I was first introduced to Freddie by my friend Deb Krainin. She met Pierre and Freddie in the Chiloé Archipelago off the coast of Chile in the town of Ancud. They were staying in the same little hotel and they all went to see the penguins together. They stayed together during their travels on the island and later they met up again in Santiago before they went on with their travels. This was in 2008 during a time when Freddie and Pierre took a yearlong world tour. Before this, in 2006, she and Pierre traveled on safari to northern Tanzania.

For her, Tanzania was a kind of Eden. A paradise. Both she and Pierre love animals, and in Tanzania you can witness the migration of millions of animals crossing the river between Tanzania and Kenya to find food and water. They saw wild buffalo, elephants, lions, leopards, and wildebeests. *"Oh, and to see them in their natural habitat—it was a life-changing experience,"* she adds. *"All of us cried at certain places."*

MEETING THE MAASAI

"This is where I met Olee, a Maasai guide. I remember it was at sunset," Freddie explains as the waiter brings a bottle of Bordeaux to the table. *"We had been traveling all day and Olee wanted to take me for a little walk. Pierre encouraged me, and so Olee took me by the hand to climb up a* kopije. *It's like a big rock. We stood there, side by side, looking out at this vast landscape, and something changed for me. I looked down at the land and I could feel a magnetic, spiritual force."*

Freddie tastes the wine and gives the waiter a nod of approval before he pours it into our wineglasses. Freddie and I toast to our health and to Tanzania. She smiles. *"You know, at the time, I didn't give this experience all that much importance. It wasn't until only later that I realized something sacred had happened and in that moment my life changed forever."*

I must stop and muse on this, how often this sort of thing happens—you are in a new place and you know what you are experiencing is important, but oftentimes, it's not only months but even years later that you realize the encounter, the experience, the little thing someone says to you is actually life-changing and will live within your heart forever, and more than this, will lead you through a doorway that you never even knew existed and take you into a completely new direction.

Perhaps you can't afford to take a yearlong trip around the world or go to Tanzania like Freddie and Pierre, but you *can* go someplace new. You can do something that is different and will help you see your world through new eyes.

And when you do this, a whole new world opens before you, as well as the possibility of a new career.

This is what happened to Freddie.

As it turns out, this Maasai guide, Olee, could speak English, and after the trip, they kept in contact by e-mail.

Freddie returned to Paris, and, inspired by her trip, she went back to university. In 2009, she received her master's degree in tourism, culture, communications, and museums.

Today, Freddie is the French partner with Soaring Flamingo, a travel company that brings visitors to beautiful Tanzania.

Freddie tells me:

"This is the magic of travel: meeting someone at the end of the world that will guide you through your life path. Maasai spirituality can be reflected in these lines of action: to overcome fears, to remain connected, to not create division within and around oneself, to make the most of life's challenges, and to experience what is."

Before the evening ends, we talk about America and I confess that sometimes I worry that the French don't like us. I do know that this is how some of my compatriots feel. And then there was that whole business with renaming French fries "freedom fries." Perhaps you remember. (Truth is, as the French will tell you, French fries are actually a Belgian invention.)

Freddie tells me, *"We love Americans! You freed us."* She smiles at me and for a moment she really does look exactly like Amélie. *"You gave us Glenn Miller."*

Freddie explains to me that her first visit to the United States was as an exchange student at Ohio State University, or *"Ooooh-high-oooh!"* she tells me. *"It was one of the best experiences of my life!*

"It was my first contact with American culture. I appreciated the way people in America live. For example, they queue and stay in line while waiting for the bus. People respect each other." She gives me the sweetest, most sincere look and leans forward. *"I discovered this in Columbus. People in the United States respect the rules."*

Really? We do?

But here you see it—how there's nothing quite like looking at your daily life from an outsider's point of view.

This is ultimately what travel brings to you—the gift of seeing your own little corner of the world, your own ordinary life, with new eyes and new appreciation. This will change you forever. And it will lead you to love, because your heart and eyes are truly open.

> **TRAVEL HELPS YOU SEE YOUR OWN WORLD WITH NEW EYES AND NEW APPRECIATION.**

Parisian Charm School Lesson

French women will tell you it's important to start traveling when you're young. You don't need a ton of money. If you're a student, look for exchange opportunities in high school and college. Look at the French Consulate site. They have quite a number of opportunities for people under thirty-five years of age. Volunteer!

Do you have family in your ancestral home? Look into visiting them. Create your own cultural exchange program.

Any kind of travel is a way to meet another culture, even if that culture is the one to be found on the other side of town. Travel is also about meeting yourself. You have to adapt to a new situation and you develop your ability to change.

Not all French women travel around the world, the way that Freddie and Pierre did. In fact, about half of French people don't travel outside of France. They'll take their five weeks of holiday and stay home, go to all the exhibitions, go to the beach, and play the tourist in their own town, and they'll visit family and friends in the country.

Many singles and married couples will rent a big house together in Brittany or the South of France.

The point is that time is meant to be savored and enjoyed. Hence, the French take off the entire month of August for their summer holidays, as well as most of December. In addition to this, the French have many more holidays where shops are closed, and the French will take time to enjoy a trip or a visit with their families.

All this might not be possible in our workaday world, but certainly, we can do more with our two- or three-week vacations. We can travel! In fact, this is one of the most important French secrets to finding love and romance, as well as a renewed sense of happiness.

If we become shut in by our own surroundings, we close ourselves off from the world both physically and intellectually, and we become set in our ways, believing that our future husband is within a ten-block radius of where we live (not to say that this isn't possible). Even if you do meet your future husband in your own neighborhood, consider that there is something very compelling about a woman who has just returned from a sojourn to an exotic locale. Perhaps you're wearing a pair of interesting earrings that you bought during your travels. You've formed new opinions about world economics. You're full of interesting stories— and maybe you've got a great tan!

Parisian Charm School Pratique

Find ways to travel by taking short trips to new places. Visit your hometown and reconnect with old friends and family. Be willing to be surprised by the unexpected person or place. Travel with new eyes and an open heart.

Read travel guides. Look at travel magazines and dream. It doesn't cost anything to dream!

You'll see. You will visit a place in a foreign land. You will find true love, or at the very least, you will make a friend and that friend will come visit you one day in America and will show you what is special about you and she will sing the praises

Travel with new eyes and an open heart.

of the humble American BLT or whatever ordinary and over-looked beauty stands for in your own precious life.

So today's lesson is to simply appreciate the ordinary daily gifts found in your own very simple but very special life.

And then make plans to see the world!

CHAPTER FIVE

Flower Power

If you have a library and a garden,
you have everything you need.
—CICERO

A RIVER RUNS THROUGH IT

I have taken the RER train from Gare d'Austerlitz to St. Martin D'Estampes, just outside of Paris, and now I am in the little village of Saclas. As I walk out of the train and down the stairs, I notice how even here in this little village there's a garden of colorful flowers arranged to greet arrivals.

I am here in Saclas to visit my Canadian friends Christian and Kathryn Kemp-Griffin. This region, the Beauce Plains between the Seine and Loire Rivers, has such a rich *terroir* and is known as the Breadbasket of France.

Saclas is still today very much an agricultural community. In fact, the first time I came to visit Kate, it was during the annual potato harvest. There was a sudden downpour of rain, and I remember standing at the doorway to the main house next to the clay pots of bright red geraniums, when I was amazed to see two strikingly handsome teenage boys running through the rain, barefoot and laughing—wearing nothing but their underpants! Honestly, they looked like an ad for Abercrombie & Fitch. These young men turned out to be Kate and Christian's sons, home from university for the summer, and they explained how they had just returned from a day of harvesting potatoes for the local farmer. They didn't want to track all the mud into the house, so they took off their clothes as soon as they entered the gate. This scene has always stayed with me because I found the moment was natural and enchanting and, well, iconic.

Kate and Christian are both from Canada. Whenever I walk around the village and people want to know how I came to be there, all I have to do is say, *I'm with the Canadians*, and everyone knows exactly where I am staying. *Oh yes, those crazy Canadians with the blue shutters!* Actually, they don't say that last part, but Kate has told me the locals seem a little distressed by the fact that their mill home has shutters in a *Provence* shade of blue when here they are in the north! *Mon dieu!* These things are important. The shutters are supposed to be a dark burgundy in the north, but Kate assured me it's not their fault. The shutters were blue when they bought the house.

Kate and Christian met at Princeton University, married and moved to France in 1990. Then in 2000 they bought their converted mill house and moved to Saclas. Christian works in the fashion industry and has been involved in a lot of business ventures that take him around the world. Kate and Christian have been married for twenty-eight years and so they have that sense of natural flow and ease you see in couples who have been together for a long time.

Still, I can tell that Kate has a way of keeping Christian on his toes. She is, after all, a lingerie expert! In fact, Kate's new book, *Paris Undressed,* has just been released and she's planning her big book tour. Kate has been a lingerie expert for many years and she's the founder of Paris Lingerie Tours and Pink Bra Bazaar.

THE SECRET GARDEN PARTY

Kate tells me I am lucky to be visiting her on this particular weekend, because today is the day of the Secret Garden (*Secret de Jardin en Essonne*) party. I have no idea what to expect from the Secret Garden Party. Actually, it would seem that this particular party is so secretive that it looks like there's no one home. We walk up to the big iron gate and Kate tries pushing it open, but it's locked. She tries ringing the bell and we wait. *Some party*, I muse. However, in true French style, after a while, in her own good time, a middle-aged lady appears. She smiles shyly and opens the gate for Kate and me, as well as the little crowd that has gathered outside. She beckons us to come and explore the gardens around her home. I don't recognize this woman's accent, and Kate explains that she's actually Russian.

Kate and I first take our tour of the gardens. We follow a little *Hansel and Gretel*–style path through a small forest of pine trees, turn a corner to find the apple trees and even a cluster of bamboo trees. There are surprises along the way—big piles of chopped wood for the fireplace, wild daisies with pale purple petals, and then we come upon a sun-filled clearing where we walk around a pond. I begin to lose all sense of direction. We walk over a wooden bridge and then another, across some overgrown patches of flowers and stone ruins and ancient steps leading who knows where, maybe some place special back when the Romans lived here and built the Roman Road back in 300 BC.

And then suddenly, we come out onto an expansive and lush green lawn with a kind of gingerbread-style cottage with burgundy shutters and crumbling stone steps at the top of a sloping hill. There on the stone wall is a little sign, LE PARADIS VERT (The Green Paradise). I stand before a wildflower garden and look at all the black-eyed Susans, wild roses, miniature daisies, and purple foxgloves, but I'm particularly enamored with the orange pods that look kind of like miniature pumpkins or jack-o'-lanterns. A French woman leans into me and whispers to me in a breathy voice, *"Ah, la cage d'amour"* (the cage of love).

There isn't much time to discuss this, because our hostess, the Russian lady, appears.

As we walk to the little makeshift "theater" and gather our red folding chairs, Kate explains that the Russians are actually brother and sister and that their late mother and father arrived here as children sometime in 1930s. So they were born here in France and are French. And now, with about twenty of us gathered around, the brother introduces himself and his sister, who apparently has a terrible cold and explains that she's very cranky. She looks at him, pretending to be annoyed, but really more bemused, and then I realize this teasing is all part of their routine. They are dressed in Russian costumes—traditional white embroidered *kosovorotka* shirts and Russian scarves. The show begins and the brother plays the balalaika and sings a traditional Russian folk song, while his cranky/bemused sister with the bad cold sings the chorus along with him and plays the guitar. I must add here that, despite her cold, she has a surprisingly beautiful singing voice.

In between songs, they banter and complain about each other, as if they are still children, and in fact, they introduce a new song and explain that it's based on the Russian folk tale, *The Cat, the Thrush, and the Cockerel.* As the sister explains it, the song is sung from the viewpoint of a fox, and he wants to steal the rooster. The audience is delighted, but suddenly we are all distracted by an actual cat on the roof of the brother and sister's cottage. Yes, their tabby/Siamese mix cat has leapt to the very apex of the roof and is padding across the peak, as if doing a high-wire circus act, demanding our full attention. Kate and I look at each other and register concern—*Is the cat going to fall off the roof?!* The brother laughs at this and surrenders the moment to the cat and her high-wire act.

The entire experience is strangely enchanting.

A CHARMING BOUQUET OF WATERCRESS

By the time we return to Kate's home, Christian has returned from his race. The annual Boucle de La Juine, which begins and finishes in Saclas, is a seven-kilometer marathon that's been going on for many, many years, and Christian always runs in it. The race goes through the village of Méréville, which prides itself as the world capital of watercress. Yes, watercress. Or *cresson*, as the French call it. The French take a great deal of pride in their watercress, and so Christian, a bit flushed and sweaty, having run the race, now proudly presents his prize—a bouquet of watercress!

It is such a simple prize, and yet elegant and practical. Christian tells me he plans to prepare a salad with his prize, mixing it in a vinaigrette dressing, adding some pine nuts, small pieces of nectarines, some walnuts, and then finally serving it with warm goat cheese.

All these things are so lovely, without being fancy. The Secret Garden party was something that appeared to have been pulled together at the last moment. The truth is, when you have nature in the leading role, your life will be effortlessly elegant. And you don't have to live in a little village outside of Paris to enjoy the charms of nature. Nature is always there for us, everywhere.

MARILYN MONROE IN THE GARDEN OF EDEN

I have arrived in Auvillar, a little village in the southwest of France, for my artist residency at the Virginia Center for the Creative Arts. I am here to write and see friends. I've stayed in Auvillar many times, but this is the first time I've noticed that the farmer next door to the VCCA at the Le Jardin du Port (the Garden of the Port) has a series of stakes with hand-painted pictures of pretty women. Most of them look very French, with hats and scarves, but then I notice that Marilyn Monroe is there, and she's right next to Elizabeth, the queen of England. *What is this all about?* you ask. Well, the good citizens of Auvillar mark their little patch of paradise by using tall stakes and signs with painted faces on the signs.

So, I imagine, it goes something like this: a French person will say, *You see the blond, red-lipsticked image of Marilyn guarding the red ripe tomatoes over there in the middle of the garden? That's my space.*

I love returning to Auvillar, because the town is considered one of France's most beautiful villages. This is an official designation by the French government. Moulin à Nef is en route to Saint-Jacques-de-Compostelle, so from my studio window, I can catch a glimpse of the pilgrims on their way to Spain. Some of them will walk with walking sticks, and there are even a few who bring donkeys with them. They stay over in the *gîtes* (little hotels) at the top of the hill in the town square, by St. Pierre, the eleventh-century cathedral.

And so here I am, writing and researching in Auvillar. I am the only nonfiction writer among the poets. There are three poets here—two from England and one from California, Susan Gubernat. Susan is a very well-published poet whose books have won many prizes. She's also an accomplished opera librettist and a professor at Cal State East Bay.

However, that's not what first caught my attention about Susan. It was her bright red lipstick!

There's this kind of unspoken sisterhood among women who wear bright red lipstick, like I do, like Susan does—and I think that's why we became instant friends. Oh, that and the fact that she's one heck of great cook!

On Sunday, everyone goes to the Auvillar market, where you can find fresh vegetables, eggs, cheese, butter, yogurt, and foie gras from the local farmers, along with very pretty flowers.

On one particular Sunday, Susan cannot go to the market, so she sends me with the mission to buy some flowers to liven up her writing studio. There are so many flowers to choose from at the market on this particular day—sweet little bouquets of red rosebuds, big white blooms of peonies, daisies, and the showgirl of French flowers: the gladiolas, with their layers of ruffled white petals, dancing in the autumn breeze. Regardless, I am drawn to the humble zinnias. Well, maybe not so humble. They are wildly colorful—hot pink, and orange, and red. When I give them to her, her eyes well up with tears. Little did I know that these were her grandmother's favorite flowers and that this bouquet of zinnias, grown in a little village in southern France, bring the spirit of Susan's grandmother into the room with us. And now, looking at the vibrant colors, the insouciant petals—I, too, can feel the courage and power and faith that bloomed in the heart of this immigrant lady, and in her garden, as well.

Recently, Susan told me the history of her grandmother and the zinnias:

"My grandmother had become an urban gardener once she arrived in America, but her background was from a farm in Galicia in Eastern Europe. And she recounted to us how they once lived on the second story of a little farmhouse where the animals resided on the first floor. Suffice it to say, she had the greenest of thumbs; she made anything flourish in that poor soil in Newark. Besides the beautiful roses, she grew a riot of multicolored zinnias—magenta, orange, bright yellow. In fall, when the flowers died, she would deadhead them and save the seeds for the year's next planting. So the zinnias were propagated, year after year, without resorting to a seed catalog; during the winter months, a shoe box held the wonderful potential of zinnias that would perk up in late summer and which I'd always connect with my own early August birthday.

"I love zinnias; they aren't dainty or well behaved. I love their wild beauty and hardiness. I loved how my grandmother's husbandry led to such bounty every year."

FLOWERS AND THE
ART OF FLIRTATION

Two years ago, while I was in Paris, I was walking down Rue Racine when I came upon two French women in front of a restaurant/café. They were huddled over a little table, speaking with great enthusiasm and even urgency, and since I am the curious type, I stopped and looked to see what was going on. As it turned out, the restaurant had left yesterday's flowers out on the table in front with a little message, inviting anyone to take some. The ladies told me that they had collected a few and that I should help myself. These were beautiful flowers—enormous pink lilies with a heady fragrance. And since I was on my way to see my friend Sylvie, I thought—*I'll bring her these lilies as part of my hostess gift.*

However, this gave me a little problem. I couldn't just show up at her door with these bare stalks of lilies, and so I went to the papeterie near Boulevard Saint-Germain. A flurry of excitement came my way the moment I walked in the door. Yes, my lilies created quite a sensation. Everyone, from the man at the door, to the customers bustling about, along with the very tall clerk, admired them.

When I asked the clerk to help me find some wrapping paper and ribbon for my lilies, well, he was more than thrilled to help me, and he also wanted me to know that if I was not careful, the pollen might come off on my dress, and then it's very difficult to remove. He described how I needed to prevent this, while another charming man—a customer—agreed.

For a moment, I made a mental note—*lilies are like catnip to men, and I must tell all my female friends about this discovery!*

This was only the first of many encounters with admiring men and women on my way down Boulevard Saint-Germain. It seemed as if I had discovered the perfect subterfuge for flirtation. Everyone admired the bouquet of pink lilies and everyone wanted to tell me about the pollen, and a few men wanted to know where I was taking those lilies and if I could possibly consider giving the flowers to them.

Ah, *amour.*

However, it wasn't *amour!* It was just some pretty flowers.

But, since I am a writer, specifically in the business of helping my readers find romance and love, let's deconstruct these lilies. Why did they cause such a sensation? Well, these were beautiful pink lilies, and so they drew attention and invited comment. In addition to this, these lilies were so big and spectacular, they created a certain curiosity around me. But here's the part that I think is important to note: because of the issue of possible pollen problems, they encouraged the *Mr. Fix-it Hero* that resides in the heart of all good men. You see, I had inadvertently stumbled on a trifecta of flirtation:

- The flowers were very pretty, and therefore worthy of compliments.
- They were so large and showy, they drew attention and created curiosity.
- The issue of the pollen pulled at the heart of heroic men who wanted to rescue me from the possible

dangers of pollen problems and thus initiate a
conversation. This pollen issue gave the men an
opportunity to show off their knowledge of pollen,
science, fabric, and stain removal, and therefore
impress me.

So there you have it—the power of flowers! It's the universal
power of nature.

PINK LILIES, TURQUOISE WALL,
AND A LEFT BANK GIRL

Without once staining myself with the pollen, I managed to
carry the lilies, unharmed, to Sylvie's apartment overlooking the
metro Maubert—Mutualité. I climbed up the five flights and
she answered the door, happy to see me. Her eyes were bright
and gleaming, her hair cropped short. She was thinner than I
remembered when she visited with us on the Cape, but she assured me that she was fine.

Sylvie took the lilies from me and put them in a big vase of
fresh water. Together, we arranged them on her mantel, in front
of a wall she had painted a beautiful deep turquoise blue. The
pink lilies truly stood out in contrast to the turquoise, and I took
a photograph of the tableau. I am glad I took that photo, because that was to be the last time I visited Sylvie in her Left
Bank apartment. And like Susan with her zinnias, I will never
look at flowers the same ever again. My dear French friend is
gone now, but whenever I am in nature, whenever I look at the
elegant pink lily or the humble daisy, I will remember Sylvie
and the special time we had together.

Parisian Charm School Lesson

Here's the truth—we can find love—not by a formula, or an algorithm, or a five-hundred-point online questionnaire, but rather by getting in touch with our own sensory responses, by enjoying life, and by being a part of whimsical everyday magic. Walk down the street carrying a big bouquet of flowers or a lace parasol, or a guitar or basket of apples, or a puppy! Be alive and present and vulnerable to the world around you.

> **Be alive and present and vulnerable to the world around you.**

In this way, like the French, the man we fall in love with might be a complete surprise and fulfill absolutely none of the items on our checklist for the perfect mate. He might just be a man who knows how to remove flower pollen from a white shirt. And he might be more perfect for us than we could ever have imagined.

Take a day where you get into conversations with men you would normally not consider romantic material. Take notice of your feelings, your sensory responses. Daydream about a man you may have rejected in the past because he just didn't look good on paper.

Ask yourself what kind of men do you truly find compelling—not the ones you're *supposed to* find compelling, but the men in your past or present who truly moved you. Is it possible that you've overlooked something in your search for perfection?

Embrace the power of flowers. Give flowers, pin a fresh

flower to your blouse, wear one in your hair, and grow flowers. Get into conversations everywhere you go.

Bring nature inside every day; even in the coldest winter months, you can put a little piece of evergreen on your mantelpiece. If you live in the city, you can buy flowers at your local market, or you can go to the supermarket and buy some lovely blooms.

PLANT SEEDS. NURTURE THEM. MIRACLES WILL BLOOM.

Parisian Charm School Pratique

Go out in nature today. Even if you live in a big city, you can take a walk in the park.

Spend some time looking at the vegetables at the market. Really look at them. Appreciate the complicated simplicity of nature. Appreciate the beauty and the miracle of the humble watercress (or basil or cilantro or thyme).

Pick some wildflowers and bring them inside. If it's not possible to pick your own flowers, then buy some at a local market and bring them into your home. This simple gesture can make all the difference in the world.

CHAPTER SIX

The Color Wheel

If a man identifies a woman with a color,
every time he sees that color, the man will
think of her and then will think of his feelings for her.
—MARINE BORDOS, DUVELLEROY, PARIS

WHO SAYS PARISIANS WEAR ONLY BLACK?

Here I am in Paris and all I see is yellow. *Yellow!* It appears to be the color for the fall season. When I ask my American expat friend Nancy, she says, *"It's like they all get a text message or something."* Nancy is married to a French doctor and has been living in Paris for over twenty years. *"Aren't you on the text message list?"* I ask her, and she laughs because we are old friends and we developed a certain banter when we first met in our twenties at Estée Lauder. This was during the launch of the iconic fragrance *Beautiful* in the bright pink packaging.

But, back to the text message. *"No,"* Nancy tells me, feigning disappointment. *"The Parisiennes have left me off the new color alerts!"*

"*C'est domage,*" I say—*It's a shame*—and she agrees.

We are enjoying our crazily expensive coffees around the corner from the fashionable Trocadero, because it's near Nancy's office and home and it does provide excellent fashion-people-watching. Nancy is still in the beauty business, while I have returned to what was always my true love: writing. And this is why I am here once again in Paris. I generally visit the City of Light twice a year, but during this particular visit, I am obsessed with color! Perhaps because it happens to be Fashion Week and I am hyperaware of the newest trends in the store windows and on the streets. Also, I think it's because I see all this yellow. Yellow coats, yellow shoes, yellow scarves, yellow pocketbooks.

My friend Edith says this is because it's autumn, the harvest season, and of course yellow is in vogue, as is burgundy for the wine and grape harvest. She tells me that for the French, fashion is always connected to nature, food, fragrance, and the land, but still—why so much yellow? Why now?

I am still puzzled by this when I meet with my Parisian friend Valerie. She does not wear this season's yellow. She wears orange. Actually, no matter what the season's "text message" happens to say, she always wears orange. It's her signature color.

Valerie is the owner of Ma Collection Marchande de Saveurs, a charming boutique in Paris, that specializes in curated gourmet delicacies (meaning she personally selects what she will feature in her store).

If you visit her shop, you will never forget Valerie. Yes, her signature color is orange. Her little boutique bags are orange. The walls in her shop are orange—and Valerie, herself, wears orange on a daily basis, including orange eyeglasses and bright red hair. It's not wild-looking at all. It's actually striking and stylish and completely enchanting. This love for the color orange is the way she brands herself. And if you think about it, the French understood the power of color and branding long before it became so in vogue. Just think about Hermès orange.

Her signature color is a simple way to convey the fact that she's fun, she's artistic, and she's an original—without saying a word about it.

> ## CHOOSE YOUR OWN SIGNATURE COLOR AND WEAR A BIT OF IT EVERY DAY.

When I ask Valerie how she came to choose this color, she smiles shyly, and then tells me with her very adorable French accent, *"Orange is an energy color. Red is too much like blood."* She takes a moment to look out the window on her shop on Rue Mazarine and then turns to me. *"Orange matches many things,"* she says with great sincerity. *"Orange is for every girl—fashion, for hair, for me—it's very elegant. It's good for a funny girl. Or maybe just a touch—a belt. It's nice for older women. Even total orange. All the time! Not just for a season!"*

I have never heard an American girl talk about a color with this level of passion. I do know that some of this passion comes from the fact that Valerie is French and English is her second language, and so her struggle to find the right words adds to this sense of urgency, a desire to be understood. (I just wanted to point that out to those of you who struggle with your French language skills—what you perhaps don't realize is that your very struggle reveals a kind of passion and energy—so try to speak French! You must!)

Valerie explains that there are also lots of shades of orange. There's brown orange. And there's yellow orange. You can match orange with green for summer. *"And it's not true that Paris is only a city of gray!"* she insists. *"There is the sunset over the Seine River. Just stand on Pont Neuf at six or seven o'clock and watch the sunset. It is such a beautiful shade of orange."*

Valerie goes on to describe her first major move to orange, when she was eighteen and she changed her hair color from blond to orange. (I would actually call her a redhead or auburn.) She says emphatically that she'll never change it back because it gives her so much energy.

"I don't like gray/blue. It's too relaxing. Orange gives me energy and makes me happy. Life is not so easy, so I'm not like a yoga girl. I work a lot. I see my friends and family. I'm a true Parisian."

Valerie tells me how she grew up in Paris. Her mother is from Normandy and her father is from England. In Paris, she loves the good food and the friendships.

We talk about her shop and why it's so popular. Valerie explains how Parisian kitchens are no longer separate spaces, like in the old days, but rather their homes will feature open kitchens where everyone gathers. *"It's less formal,"* Valerie explains—and lovely for potlucks. Everyone helps in the kitchen.

When I ask her about the olive oil she sells in the shop and how the bottle has a spritz and actually looks more like expensive perfume than olive oil, she tells me that she believes in good quality and good style.

Valerie tells me that as a child, she loved candies. She would visit Madame Gentille *(Madame Sweet).* She actually doesn't remember the lady's real name, but as a child she called her this because she loved Madame Gentille's caramels, jelly candies, and lollipops. She found the shop so enchanting, that she thought when she grew up, she would buy the shop. Well, years went by and Valerie went to the famous French fashion school the École supérieure des arts et techniques de la mode (ESMOD), and it was there she learned the fine art of lingerie design. You see, from loving candies and bonbons to an appreciation of lace and silk, ribbons and bows—that froufrou—well, it makes perfect sense, doesn't it?

Valerie stops to talk to a customer who has entered her shop. The woman is here to buy truffle olive oil, and a lively conversation ensues about cooking and dinner parties and how a good truffle olive oil isn't too strong, but has just the essence of truffle inside it. She adds that this truffle olive oil should be used during the next six months and to be careful not to expose it to light or sunshine.

When Valerie finishes the sale, she returns to our conversation and tells me that she recently traveled to China for a customer where she gave a talk on the latest color trends in Paris and matched lingerie with certain foods. I repeat what she's just told me to make sure I'm hearing right. *"You match lingerie with certain foods?"*

"Of course!" she says, looking slightly impatient. *"Lingerie and flavor—it is the same thing. Sensuality of lingerie is the same as sensuality of food."*

SIXTY SHADES OF GRAY

Carol Gillott and I have known each other for many years. We met in New York City, originally, because we're both devoted Francophiles and because I just really wanted to meet the creator of one of my very favorite blogs, *Parisbreakfast*. Take a look. Carol's byline is "I paint Paris dreams." Carol is a wonderful artist who chose travel over marriage, or so she tells me, but you never know. I have a feeling there will be love in her future, because she is so charming and so talented. Before she became a full-time blogger in 2006, Carol designed shoes in Italy and fashion in Hong Kong. She created wine artwork for a leading New York City wine company and spent her holidays in Veuve Clicquot's mansion in Verzy and various châteaux in Bordeaux.

What a life!

And then, in 2012, at age seventy-two, Carol moved to Paris full-time. She tells me it was to save on airfare. She's funny like that. And she doesn't look her age. She has a strawberry blond pixie cut, signature red eyeglasses, and green eyes. Oh, and she tells me she wears MAC Russian Red lipstick. (Note to self: must try out that shade.) She's very gamine and looks to be in her early fifties, if that. Today, she lives on the historic Île Saint-Louis in her artist's garret, a *chambre de bonne* (top-floor maid's room) in an historic mansion. She looks out on a stunning view across Paris while she's painting and illustrating letters and maps that she then sends out to her devoted subscribers around the world.

Yes, she's the quintessential artist and knows her colors. That's for sure.

We are having lunch on a particularly gray Parisian day at the oldest restaurant in Paris, Café Procope on Rue de l'Ancienne Comédie. We order the canard (duck) and two flutes of champagne.

I ask Carol what's going on with color in Paris. She gives me an earful. I ask her why the basic fashion palette in Paris is either gray or black, and she tells me that it's because of the light in Paris. She gives me a knowing smile. *"They don't call it* le ville de lumière *for nothing!"* And then, on a more serious note, she deconstructs Paris gray for me.

"It's the gray skies, and all that drizzle, the gray/buff neutral tones of the Haussmann buildings and the gray cobblestone streets. It has nothing to do with genetics or Marie Antoinette, and everything to do with the weather.

"Why have artists always loved Paris and flocked here? Colors are richer with overcast skies. Photographers prefer overcast gray skies because they get more reflected color that way.

"Gray skies make vibrant colors sing. It's basic color theory. Gray acts as the perfect foil for brilliant colors. It's why you see shots of bright blue or yellow or red storefronts in Paris.

Gray skies make vibrant colors sing.

"Brilliant colors and strong colors radiate against this serene gray backdrop. We adore Ladurée's *pale green, Veuve Clicquot's yellow champagne label,* Hermès's *orange bags,* Hediard's *red,* Fauchon's *hot pink.*

"All chocolatiers adore orange. In fact, orange is a very hot color in Paris. It connotes class and luxe and stands out against black fashions."

I tell Carol about Valerie and she smiles enthusiastically and adds that orange is also a signature color for Hermès and the annual *Salon du Chocolat.*

"Parisians seek out brilliant color, but it has to be just the right shade—because they live in a mostly gray environment. They need color to breathe, exist."

Then Carol tells me, *"As an outsider, or an extraterrestrial"*—she laughs—*"I can see what the French don't see."*

We clink our champagne flutes together in a toast and pronounce, *"À la votre!"*

HERE COMES THE SUN

If you were in Paris this past winter, you would have found a series of large posters in the metro stations and on the streets advertising winter getaways to sunny climes. Surprisingly, the posters do not feature a beach scene in Aruba or St. Maarten, but rather a colorful photograph of the Château de Versailles, displaying hot pink furniture and luxurious hot pink drapes. The ad says:

> *Cet hiver, prenez des couleurs.*
> *Cet hiver, changez d'horizon.*
> *Prenez le soleil.*
> *Changez d'itineraire.*

To translate: *This winter, think color. This winter, change your horizon. Take the sun. Change your itinerary.* For me, this is a revelation. Suppose I can't manage a vacation to an island or even a trip to sunny Florida. I can still afford to "think color." I can go to a museum. I can still wear a hot pink scarf.

CHANGE YOUR MOOD AND
EVEN YOUR FUTURE BY
CHANGING YOUR COLOR.

FEELING BLUE

When I travel throughout France, I can see that this attention to color is a big deal. How is it that French women seem to have a natural gift for choosing their signature color?

Denise is an artist and great champion for the color blue. I first met her in 2010 when I was in Auvillar teaching a creative writing workshop alongside the artist Cheryl Fortier, who was teaching a watercolor workshop. We took our students on a field trip to Bleu de Lectoure to learn about the woad plant and how the color blue was created in the middle ages. Denise is a petite woman with very short hair and penetratingly blue eyes. As she stood before a huge vat of blue dye, stirring the rich liquid with a wooden paddle, I couldn't help but think of her as a very wise woman with a strong connection to French history. And indeed, she mesmerized the audience of writers and artists with tales of how the color blue was brought into being from the little woad plant. She held up the soft green petals and then passed them through the crowd for all of us to examine, as she continued to enrapture us with her stories of France during the fifteenth and sixteenth centuries.

I was so taken by the experience and stories that day that I bought a hand-dyed blue beret in the gift shop and have embraced blue ever since as my signature color. After this I will never take the color blue (or any color for that matter) for granted again, because I now see how much work and struggle and passion has gone into its creation.

Denise's new workshop is in Montjoi, near Auvillar, and is open for public visits. She was actually born in America, raised in France by parents who surrounded her with classical music and European history. She and her late husband fell in love with the southwest of France and they fell in love with French blue. She became a woad master and over the years they worked and were able to create some of the most exquisite shades of blue. My beret is an example of her one-of-a-kind blues. No one in the world will ever have the same blue beret as me, because it has certain flaws that make it completely original.

Today, I ask Denise how is it that French women seem to have this natural knack for appreciating and choosing colors, and she explains that it's all about history and tradition and symbolism:

"For many centuries colors had significance in terms of your social status, as well as your geographical location. A woman would choose a specific color depending on the time of the day, the year, her marital status, and her love status. In the court of France, where you had to be a fashion icon, if the king's favorite wore a light shade of blue, that meant something, as well as wearing a pale red or a rich gold yellow. There was a code to respect. And this code

was always handed down from mother to daughter, no matter if you were rich or poor, whether you lived in Paris or in the provinces. Dress codes were dictated by the colors.

"I think that this understanding of color has remained with the French women. French women have always shown a certain innate ability to choose the color that makes them beautiful, making them almost always chic. Like Italy, France is a country of colors, **For the French woman, color is used to seduce.** *in art, in history, and in decoration. The little girl learns from watching her mother, who looks at paintings and the different colors in nature. I truly believe that it is something inherent now. In France, seduction is important, and for the French woman, color is used to seduce. French women have lots of imagination and do not hesitate to use bright colors to enhance their looks."*

NEVER BE AFRAID OF BRIGHT COLORS.

I am very moved by Denise's thought that mothers and daughters look at paintings together. They look at the colors in nature. I raised a young artist. She's now thirty-three years old and has a daughter of her own, but I often think about how when she was just a little girl and I was studying screenwriting at UCLA School of Theatre, Film and Television, she would accompany me for the day. We wandered through the sculpture

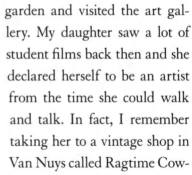

garden and visited the art gallery. My daughter saw a lot of student films back then and she declared herself to be an artist from the time she could walk and talk. In fact, I remember taking her to a vintage shop in Van Nuys called Ragtime Cowboy, and they just happened to be having a sale on ballerina tutus. They were one dollar each, and we bought ten of them in a rainbow of colors.

Today, my daughter is a mother to little Junie, and a graphic designer. And she has a great eye for color! It's exactly what Denise says. An appreciation and understanding of color is handed down from mother to daughter. So, if that's the case, why not begin today? Take a walk in nature and notice the colors of the sky and the trees. Go to the museum and look for colors that feel meaningful to you. Ask yourself what colors create a kind of invisible thread between you and your ancestors. You might not quite understand why that particular shade of soft coral or even that vivid stroke of magenta makes you suddenly release a deep sigh, but I suggest you trust your instincts. Trust your body and your emotions when it comes to color, because this is how your ancestors, your grandmother and great-grandmother and great-great-grandmother, are talking to you, through time and space, and history.

Take a moment and listen to the sound that color makes in your heart.

Parisian Charm School Lesson

Many of us have had our "colors done," meaning we met with an expert or we read the book that describes how to choose colors that are flattering to our skin tone. It's all very pragmatic and has a certain science to it. The French will also have their "colors done" as a way of discovering what shades (autumn, winter, spring, summer) look best on them, but then French women take this knowledge to a much deeper level.

French women use their knowledge of color to find joie de vivre, beauty, peace, success, and love. Can choosing the right colors lead to love? French women will tell you, yes, *absolument!*

Practically all the French women I know have embraced the idea of a signature color. My friend Marie-Joëlle in Besançon, a university town southeast of Paris, uses color in a variety of ways—she owns a hair salon, so she's very experimental with her choices. She'll often wear shades of purple or plum, and mix it with an unexpected metallic, a silver jacket, or gold high-top sneakers. It sounds a bit wild, and it is, but it's also incredibly eye-catching and stylish. When Jessica and I stayed with her family a few years ago, I noticed how when you first walked into her home, there was a room where one wall was painted bright yellow. Marie-Joëlle had a series of hats displayed on this wall. There must have been about twenty hats, and the entire effect was really charming.

IF YOU HAVEN'T ALREADY, FIND out what color range looks best on you and then choose your signature color. More than this, explore how various colors make you feel. What gives you that feeling of changing your horizons? Ask yourself what color reflects your personality and how you want to be seen in this world. How do you want a man to remember you? When he sees the color of the sky, will he think of you? French women know that color; clothing and décor are deeply personal, and so they will go on a lifelong search for self. Even the color of their cars reflect their psyche. (By the way, you'll see lots of little cars in France with fanciful colors—pink, pale blue, orange, yellow, light green, and even turquoise.)

I have a wonderful friend in my hometown. Her name is Marianne, and I first met her at our local farmer's market, where my husband and I have a booth selling vegetables and Marianne sells wildflowers and herbal infusions. Her banner reads LE JARDIN D'ISEULT (the garden of Iseult). Her ten-year-old son is named Tristan, so you can imagine how I was immediately fascinated by this young woman and through the hot summer days of sitting at our little booths and greeting customers, we became good friends.

During the holidays, Marianne and Tristan came for dinner and we got into a conversation about my hot pink chairs. Yes, despite Dr. Thompson's protestations, we have two hot pink chairs in a kind of Louis XIV style with a fleur-du-lis print. My father said something about moving a chair and we were confused about which chair he was referring to. This is when Marianne said, *"Oh, you mean the bordello chairs?"* At first, I thought this should distress me, but I realized I kind of liked the idea. Yes, these are sexy chairs. They're hot pink and they connect with my being the daughter of a very showy lady— vaudeville/burlesque—and I am not a beige sofa kind of gal! I'm a hot pink velvet chair kind of gal, and like Valerie's orange, hot pink gives me energy. It makes me happy.

I hope this inspires you to ask yourself, *What makes me happy?* It might be a peaceful blue or the purity of white or purple. Or it might be bright orange. The point is to find your happiness.

And as an aside, men love-love-love happy women.

Consider that the color you choose is a conversation opener, as powerful as carrying a bunch of lilies down Boulevard Saint-Germaine, because when you dress in something particularly pretty and stylish and unique to your own personality, you are sending out an unspoken message that you are confident and would welcome a little lighthearted flirtation.

Parisian Charm School Pratique

This week, take a chance on a color that you love, but perhaps feel is a little *de trop* (too much). At first, just wear this color as an accessory such as a scarf. Ask yourself how it makes you feel and pay attention to how people respond to your color.

Look at nature to see what colors capture your imagination. Experiment in your home by adding colorful accents. Buy a couple of throw pillows and see how the color makes you feel and how it reacts to your home's surroundings.

Let your colors have a conversation with one another.

Do this by first separating all the clothes in your closet by color and then take them one by one and introduce each item to a contrasting mate. See what lights up your eyes and your heart.

CHAPTER SEVEN

The Art of the French Flirt

(And Why Conversation Matters)

When she raises her eyelids,
it's as if she were taking off all her clothes.
—COLETTE

WHENEVER I TALK TO AMERICAN FRIENDS about flirting, they seem to get a little nervous. Men get particularly nervous. I think this is because they imagine that flirting is a kind of sexual promise and if unfulfilled, they interpret this perceived promise as no more than a big (and extremely disappointing) tease. In fact, they actually feel they've been tricked!

On the other hand, American women want to know, *How do I get the guy?* A French woman will tell you that this is actually the wrong question. This idea of *getting the guy* is what will keep the guy away. Plus, it turns you into the one who is pursuing him, and it's much better when he's pursuing you. Truthfully, we would all be much better served by slowing down and enjoying life and love and friendship and sparkling conversation and being alive to possibility and beauty in the world.

And this is why flirting and charm are so important to French life. It's an elegant way of getting to "yes" without even asking the question. And it's a way of sharing a bit of sunshine with the world.

EARLY ON IN MY STUDIES with Madame M., she taught me that the French word for "flirt" comes from *conter fleurette,* which basically means to talk sweetly and to have a nice repartee. We might translate this as "sweet talk," but the concept of flirting is so much more subtle and complex in French. When it comes to the French flirt, there is no goal or purpose other than to bring a little charm into your daily life. French women know that when we have developed our sense of charm, along with poise, intelligence, grace, and an appreciation for the world around us, well, then we are irresistible.

French women "flirt" (talk about the flowers) all the time with everyone. French women will often make a comment about the weather or what cute shoes you're wearing or perhaps ask a question that's relevant to the moment. They might complain (this is actually a favorite pastime for the French). It's a matter of being friendly and interested in life, getting into conversations with people, and being present to

> *Charm and wit are the cornerstones of French flirting.*

the moment. Charm and wit are the cornerstones of French flirting. French women have told me that you simply can't prepare witty *bon mots* in advance of conversation, but rather you must stay on your toes and really listen, then react quickly, using your intellect. It's a little game of wits, and it's light and fun.

AND THERE'S ANOTHER BENEFIT from this—you might be *conter fleurette* with an old lady or a child, and a gentleman might overhear you and join in on the conversation. He feels safe this way. He is not harassing anyone. He is not "coming on." But rather, he is simply being interested.

A common mistake most American women make is that we try to flirt alone with a man. This really doesn't work to our advantage. It makes everyone a little nervous and, yes, this can give a guy the wrong idea. French women do things in groups— it's the way the old-fashioned idea of the chaperone has evolved in Europe. True, they don't have Jane Austen–style chaperones, but they do tend to go out in groups, and, of course, dinner parties are preferred over dating in France. Community events and parties are a wonderful way to keep your intentions mysterious. No one suspects you might have a crush on one particular man. That is your own delicious secret, to be savored and explored in your own sweet time. There are no agendas in this scenario, only pleasure and charm.

MASTER FLIRT

Now when I look back at my lessons with Madame M., I realize she was a PhD in the art of French flirtation, if there were such a thing. Truly, she was a master flirt. Before I even arrived at her front door, I could feel myself being seduced. I approached her house by driving down the long, winding path under a canopy of old trees, my car tires crunching noisily over the autumn leaves. I parked my car and then approached her door and thumped three times on the dragonfly door knocker. Sometimes she would open the door quickly and smile as if she were surprised to see me (even though she had been expecting me ten minutes ago), but then greet me like a long-lost friend, with a *bisou* on each cheek, and then she would say something sweet about my hair or my scarf or my bag.

Madame M. was always dressed beautifully. She always wore a pretty scarf and she always wore her signature Guerlain perfume. After I got to know Madame M. a little better, she would often hide behind the door, let it open slowly, and then when I called her name and pushed the door, she would peep out and say, "Boo!"

I had to laugh. Every single time she did this, I started laughing. It was just the silliest and funniest thing ever! You would think the two of us were about ten years old.

And this was just the beginning of the flirtation that went in my lessons. She would bring out books with lovely photographs of France and she often served delicious little treats—fresh strawberries that we could dip in finely granulated sugar. In the winter, she served hot tea and we would read the little messages on the tea bags and then translate them into French. Serious stuff, this learning French!

In the summer, she served iced tea that we stirred with her family's silver iced tea spoons—the ones with really skinny straws and the tiny heart on the end that served as a spoon. (You see, even her silverware was flirtatious!)

Madame M. taught me how to modulate my voice for full effect, when to whisper, and when to say nothing at all. Oh, and every once in a while, she would say something a little cheeky and then she'd wink at me. You can see why I fell under her spell. And if you deconstruct my lessons, you will see that she employed the classic art of seduction, following all these time-worn principles:

Secrecy. Yes, there was the routine of hiding behind the door, but more than this, Madame M. never let me see the mysterious private rooms of her house, where she apparently had thousands of books.

Surprise. She had a way of hiding behind the door and then suddenly peeking out, as well as the messages on the Yogi Tea.

Sound. Her voice was a musical instrument and a delight to the ears.

Smile. She used her smile to wonderful effect. Sometimes she would withhold her smile and even pretend to be quite strict. At other times, she would slay me with her sweet smile.

Style. She dressed beautifully in elegant skirts and sweaters, always with a pretty scarf tied around her neck. She always wore a bit of plum lipstick.

I do believe that this sly sense of formality might just be a cornerstone of French flirtation. You see, if we are always casual, if we are overly friendly and open and much too quick to completely reveal ourselves and give away all our secrets—well, then we have no where to go in terms of the slow dance to intimacy. If we are "intimate" all the time, then how do we create a burning desire to truly know us better? And ultimately, the slow burn is so much more desirable, *n'est-ce pas?*

FLIRTING WITH THE ÉCLAIR

I am walking down Rue de l'Ancienne-Comédie and I pass Café Procope, the restaurant where I had lunch with Carol Gillott a few weeks earlier. It's the oldest restaurant in Paris, founded in 1686, and it's always busy. It's really bustling today, and I have to scoot around a small group of customers standing outside, whispering in French, looking at the menu, then whispering some more. I continue down the street and just as I am about to turn onto Rue Dauphine, I come upon a most intriguing vision. I am standing in front of L'Éclair de Génie, and I am confused. The décor is very modern—not at all what you'd imagine a Parisian pâtisserie to look like. The color scheme is bright yellow, and honestly, when I first look inside the shop, it doesn't even register for me that this shop sells éclairs. In fact, as I watch the interaction between a nice looking man in a suit and tie and a young salesgirl, I imagine the store sells fine watches.

I step a little closer to the window and discreetly look inside. The éclairs are lined up in a perfect row as if they are expensive jewelry in a glass case. The man leans over and points to one of the delicacies. The shop girl pulls out a tray and discusses the virtues of the éclairs in question. This goes on for quite some time.

Each individual éclair is a work of art, beautifully arranged to showcase its unique appeal. Oh, and they're small and elegant, topped with luscious-looking berries and colorful bonbons.

I imagine they must be very expensive. And the most important part of enjoying one of these éclairs is the experience of coming into the store and talking with the store clerk and learning all about the assorted varieties, and the process of selecting the éclair. How could you then go home—or worse yet, walk out on the street—unwrap your prized éclair, and gobble it down? You know all about this éclair! You've discovered this éclair's history, its special appeal. You are now familiar with the nuances of this éclair. You selected this éclair out of all the other charming and delicious-looking éclairs. *Mon dieu*, it's as if you're in a relationship with this beautiful little pastry!

ALL RIGHT, STAY WITH ME here.

I think buying an éclair in Paris offers us an opportunity to learn all about the art of Parisian charm, and even more about how the French flirt.

Yes, the man and the woman are flirting. Don't ask me how I know this, but I know it, and besides, this is Paris. However, they are not talking about anything personal, but rather they are talking—passionately, I might add—about éclairs. The pair of them are having a private moment in a public space. This adds a lovely tension. They are both dressed up, so there's a feeling of formality. The man is wearing a suit and the shopgirl is wearing her official L'Éclair de Génie uniform. A large counter filled with luscious little éclairs separates them, but not too much. They are alone, but another customer could walk in on them at any moment. And of course, there's that middle-aged American woman with her camera and Moleskine notebook, trying not to be noticed as she hides at the far corner of the shop window. So you see, you have this delicious tension between public and private space. In addition to this, there is limited time. He can't stay in that shop forever, but certainly, the French take their time when it comes to selecting a dessert—and this makes sense because this particular dessert is most assuredly a work of art.

And not only that, but this éclair has provided a theatrical opportunity for the handsome man to tell an amusing story when he brings his prized box of éclairs (yes, he's buying a box of them) with him to that dinner party he will inevitably attend that evening. Ah, the stories he'll tell, and how he'll show off his newfound knowledge about éclairs and delight everyone in attendance with his brilliant insights.

That's how the French flirt.

CHAMBRE BLEUE

Paris was not always the civilized city that we know it to be today. In fact, there was a time during the early part of the seventeenth century when women were not always appreciated for their femininity and beauty and the streets were dangerous. During this time, Catherine de Vivonne, the Marquise de Rambouillet, founded the Blue Room, or *Chambre Bleue*, and Paris (and the world) changed forever. This salon elevated the art of conversation and flirtation to the highest standards. The salon included members of the royal court, as well as artists, writers, and philosophers, where important topics such as manners, poetry, literature, dance and games could be discussed through lively banter. For ladies, the salon was an opportunity to be seen and to flirt. In this heated environment, a woman's intellect and education became just as important as her style of dress and beauty. While women had very little public power in the seventeenth century, *Chambre Bleue* gave them quite a bit of power. In fact, you might call the salons the first organized charm school, because it was here that French women learned how to dress beautifully, the art of discourse, how to be graceful and witty, and how to flirt intelligently.

This is how France evolved into a culture where a woman's intellect is considered just as powerful as her beauty. This is how you get to a society that adores and respects the older, the more experienced and well-read woman—*le femme d'un certain âge.*

FLIRTING FOR SHY PEOPLE

Okay, suppose you're shy. And suppose you don't really feel comfortable participating in witty repartee *à la française.* In fact, you don't even like to complain about the weather.

Well, the French have the perfect answer for you—hide behind a fan! Peek out every now and then and flutter your eyelashes or perhaps just flash a little smile and then hide again. Seriously. It's enchanting.

I've always loved old-fashioned fans, but I had never heard of Duvelleroy, an iconic French fan designer, until I went to a lecture at my local library in Kinderhook, New York. Abbey Chase, a longtime fan aficionado, was there to give a lecture on the history of fans. I happen to have a weakness for old-fashioned costumes and accessories. In fact, I collect ladies' gloves, parasols, vintage handbags, and fans. I don't actually have a big collection by any means—certainly nothing close to the variety and size of Abbey Chase's collection! She delighted the library audience, showing us fans from all over the world—big sequin fans from 1920s music halls, silk English fans with painted scenes from the countryside, enormous ostrich feather fans, and pretty rice paper fans from the Far East.

Later, when we had an opportunity to talk, Abbey told me about the famous French fan house and how Duvelleroy had recently reopened their boutique in Paris. Of course, I made it my mission to stop by the shop on my very next visit to Paris.

17 RUE AMÉLIE, 7TH ARRONDISSEMENT, PARIS

And so here I am in Paris, standing in front of the window of Duvelleroy. The exterior of the shop is painted a bright yellow. I ring the little bell and Marine steps out to let me in. Marine is a youngish woman with long, sleek black hair. She's wearing a pair of those black-framed braniac eyeglasses and a short flirty black skirt, with black tights and black ankle boots. She smiles and welcomes me into the shop.

Honestly, it looks a bit like an art gallery. All these beautiful fans are displayed on the walls and in the store window. Marine explains to me how the owners of the shop, Eloïse and Raphaëlle, met each other on a summer day around a pool and she admired her signature fan. Both Raphaëlle and Eloïse are passionate about French heritage brands and are trained in art, marketing, and branding. This first meeting at the party led to a conversation, and once they discovered that the Duvelleroy archives were available, they jumped at the opportunity to revive this very historical house, originally founded in 1827.

As Marine gives me a peek at the archive drawer and shows me the fans, she explains the importance of the house.

"In haute couture, we are interested in the past, the history and of course, French luxury."

She picks up an enormous white ostrich feather fan and holds it in front of her face.

"In haute couture, a brand has to communicate its past because fashion changes every day. There are always new trends, and so the history is very important, because it tells us why the brand didn't disappear. If it's still here, there is a reason."

I must admit that I am yearning to own one of these haute couture fans. They're really spectacular and something you'd see onstage at a music hall in 1923. However, when I ask how much they cost, Marine tells me they're around two thousand euros. Still, a gal can dream. In the meantime, we move on to the ready-to-wear collection. They're absolutely adorable and cheeky and funny. There's one that says in big bold red letters, OH BABY! Another one, which Katy Perry famously carried at Fashion Week, says AIR-CONDITIONING. There's a sweet, very Parisian one with a picture of lipstick and the Eiffel Tower and a cat, and it says, KISS ME! And then there's another that features a picture of a Parisienne with her iPhone, taking a selfie, and it says, JE M'AIME! They're so fun. And they're only thirty-two euros.

Marine helps me select a little ready-to-wear fan with little blue tigers on it. It's very cute, but even as she is running my credit card through the machine, I am thinking, *Where am I actually going to use this fan?* And then there's the JE M'AIME! fan. Even before my blue tiger fan is in the velvet bag, I regret not buying the JE M'AIME! fan.

Marine tells me that the French always carry fans during the summer, especially on the metro. And then, there are lots of places in Paris that are not air-conditioned, so a fan is the perfect thing. And of course, French women (and lots of men) will own at least one fancy fan to bring to parties, masked balls, the theater, concerts, or any kind of gala event.

And then Marine shows me the most delightful little brochure from the archives. It's a reprint from the beginning of the nineteenth century with illustrated descriptions on the language of fans. Apparently, in the old days, a woman could secretly communicate all sorts of messages to men, just by the flick of her fan. She could tell a man that she was busy or engaged. She could encourage him to follow her. She could even ask him if he loved her, just by tapping her fan.

iPHONES, SUNGLASSES, LATTES, AND CATS

Later, I meet with my friend Mimi and I tell her about my afternoon at Duvelleroy, and I ask her what she thinks about the early nineteenth-century brochure and language of fans. Mimi gives me a knowing smile. "Well, of course they used fans to send messages. They couldn't text one another back then!"

Still, this has got me thinking. What if we could send messages with fans? I wonder if Anna Wintour would need her sunglasses and giant latte. Does she really drink that latte or does she really just carry it around as a kind of shield, as if she wants to say, *Don't get too close to me or you'll get burned by this giant latte?*

And then there are the sunglasses. They definitely serve to protect and distance.

The same goes for the creative director of Chanel, Karl Lagerfeld. He always wears sunglasses, and he used to use fans, but then he lost a lot of weight and stopped carrying a fan. But then he got a big white Persian cat named Choupette. Choupette has her own Twitter account with over fifty-one thousand followers. She considers Karl to be her father, and somehow Coco Chanel is her grandmother.

But that's not my point here. My point is that Anna Wintour and Karl Lagerfeld are geniuses at the shy person's flirt. They might not carry a hand fan, but they use their props—sunglasses, lattes, and cats—to brilliant effect.

If you are shy but aren't ready to engage in brilliant conversation, take a look at the language of everyday objects. When you lower your eyeglasses and blink your eyes, you are sending out a signal. When you hold your teacup up to your mouth and smile with your eyes alone, you are flirting. When you wear a hat and take it off, you are sending the message that you feel at home. When you slowly remove your gloves or your scarf, you are seducing. You see, you don't have to say a word to be a master flirt.

You don't have to say a word to be a master flirt.

Just get a cat! (Kidding.)

Parisian Charm School Lesson

This is why flirtation works so beautifully in France. The elegance and dignity of everyday life—the beautiful clothes, the thoughtful regard for decorum, the separation between public and private space—make the idea of approaching a woman and whistling and saying something disrespectful seem completely wrong.

If you live in a world where there is a sense of dignity, then the men around you will take a cue from you and behave appropriately. Well, maybe some won't, but you don't want to have anything to do with a guy who doesn't know how to behave. And if the men around you don't quite know how to flirt *à la française*, well, maybe they will learn, because you will teach them by example.

Redefine flirting in your own life, as a way to slow things down and prevent the one-night stand. It's not exactly a roadblock, but rather a charming detour that keeps men interested and a little uncertain about whether a woman is just sweet and friendly, or interested in something more.

Practice flirting with someone who will know you are doing nothing more than enjoying a fun conversation. Then, experiment with the very subtle flirt and take note of the responses you garner. This is a great way to gain confidence in your flirting technique.

Learn to flirt with your eyes alone. Then consider your facial expressions and how they may or may not be seductive.

Think about your own cultural history. How did your grandparents flirt? Ask your parents or grandparents how they met and courted. Browse through old family photographs for clues to your own style of flirtation. Take the time to daydream about your earliest memories of grown-ups flirting. What stands out for you and what might you bring into your own romantic life? And finally, take these pieces of memory and imagination and try them out with a spirit of curiosity and an open heart.

Parisian Charm School Pratique

This week, take a fresh look at those routine everyday encounters, such as buying stamps at the post office, and make an effort to spark simple and friendly conversations.

Practice, polish, and develop your own unique art of flirtation.

Begin using your accessories as a way to ignite a man's imagination. Take your scarf and gloves off slowly. Remove your eyeglasses, or put them on with a sense of purpose.

Everything you do can captivate and charm the world around you.

Look at everyday objects, such as a coffee cup, your iPhone, and a puppy, with this new secret knowledge that everything you do can captivate and charm the world around you.

CHAPTER EIGHT

Voice Lessons

I have found my voice again and the art of using it.
—COLETTE, FROM *THE VAGABOND*

THE FRENCH WOMAN IS A PERPETUAL MYS-
tery, and many articles and books have been written about how
she manages to keep us endlessly fascinated. You might think
her secret is her seeming insouciance—the way she ties that
Hermès scarf around her neck in a most beguiling knot. Or
perhaps you imagine her charm has something to do with her
walk and the mesmerizing click-click-click of her heels. Then
again, maybe you assume it's her knowledge of wine and food,
fashion and seduction, cinema and literature.

And you'd be close to the source of her special power, but
you'd be missing a very important key to her allure. And this is
because the real secret to a French woman's charm is very simple, very obvious, and very important.

It's the sound of her voice.

It's the power of her voice to hypnotize and seduce.

I've always felt this about the French voice, but it wasn't until I met Nicole, the creator of a concierge service called *Personal Paris,* that I truly appreciated the power and subtlety of the voice.

It's a Tuesday night, and Nicole texts me that we should meet at the Metro Abbesses in Montmartre, and then she adds that once I've arrived at the station, if I want some exercise I should take the stairs.

Being the hardworking American that I am, I am always interested in multitasking. I think, *Well, of course I'll take the stairs!*

And so I arrive at Abbesses and notice that I have two options: the elevator—and, believe it or not, there are a bunch of French people crowding into the elevator—or the stairs. The people on the elevator seem a little grouchy to me, but, ah, the people who have chosen the stairs are laughing!

I definitely want to take those stairs. And I am so glad I decided to take the long, circular route, round and round and up and up, because I am rewarded with so much more than just exercise. The walls along the steps are painted with the most beautiful murals. I step past a painting of dozens of smiling soldier boys playing the drums in red, white, and blue uniforms, wearing bright red Phrygian caps, also known as liberty caps, a reference to the French Revolution.

I round the corner along with a man and woman who hold on to each other's hands, laughing in low, sexy voices. I try to keep up, climbing up more steps, but I lose sight of them, and then I must slow down and breathe, as I come upon a big, bold abstract depicting the Moulin Rouge. And then, climbing and turning, round and round, I arrive in a kind of very blue night sky with stars and fanciful dancing white horses with wings. It feels like a dream, and I catch my breath again to turn round and round and climb up the steps, and then I find myself in front of a mural of Montmartre, with a view of the city of Paris below, and the Eiffel Tower far in the distance, as if to tell me I have come a long way from the 7th arrondissement. I am definitely in the 18th arrondissement now, home of the Sacré-Coeur. Just as the magic of Montmartre seems to take hold of my heart, I step up to an explosion of watercolor blossoms, painted in tones of rich butterscotch yellow.

Yes, the enchantment is complete, and so, by the time I take my last step and meet Nicole, I have already surrendered.

THE SOUND OF HER VOICE

This is the first thing that I notice about my new friend, Nicole, when she greets me. I can hardly concentrate on what she is saying to me—something about the rain, but I am so distracted by the beauty of her voice that I simply agree with her and follow her. Her voice isn't breathy, but it has a tonal quality that is very calming, as if she doesn't want to cause a ruckus or garner attention from the people around us. Yes, that's it. There's a slight secretive quality to her voice. I immediately feel that I am about to learn all the French secrets. Okay, maybe not all of them, but certainly a lot.

Nicole is a true Parisienne. She has worked for Chanel haute couture and Dior perfumes and makeup, and Petit Bateau, a century-old French brand that makes the famous striped Breton shirt, the "mariner." She wears a red lipstick and one of those striped Breton shirts (I assume it's from Petit Bateau) under her leather jacket and a boyish cap that gives her a certain gamine look. It's the same cap you'll see on the little boy in *Les Misérables*. "*Titi Parisienne,*" Nicole tells me, meaning "typically Parisienne." It's called a *casquette*, a typical worker's cap from the 1900s—the same iconic hat that her father wore, and her grandfather before him. Nicole tells me that this hat is a sign of freedom and rebellion.

Nicole tells me that she wants to show me a very special place that she knows I will adore. I agree and follow her up the steep hill, careful not to slip on the rained-on cobblestone streets. *"I want to show you my secret Paris."*

HÔTEL PARTICULIER

Nicole and I turn onto a street and approach what looks like the gate to a private home. She approaches the large wrought-iron door and finds a little box where she punches in some numbers, a secret code. Magically, the gate opens, and so I follow her through a lush garden, full of green flowering plants made even greener by the rain. We come to the end of the cobblestone pathway, and Nicole gestures into the night sky. *"Look,"* she says, and there in the distance, between the branches of the trees, down the hill below, peeking between the rooftops of Montmartre, is the beacon of Paris, the Eiffel Tower, lit up for the evening in golden shimmering lights. *"This is very beautiful, no?"* Nicole asks me. *"You'll want a photograph,"* she adds, reading my mind. We both take photos, knowing that this will be a lovely memento of the evening the Parisienne shared her personal Paris with this American writer.

After this, we walk down the garden path, past the terrace with white wrought-iron café tables and chairs, to a white

château with white shutters. This is the hotel/restaurant, Hôtel Particulier. It was once a wealthy French person's private home, but has been transformed. We walk up the steps, open the door, and it really does still feel as if we've entered a very fashionable private home—filled with flowers and candlelight and the melodic shushing sounds of a French chanteuse singing about love. Nicole whispers something to the young woman in the black dress—the hostess—and she motions for us to follow her. We walk through various rooms, filled with French people laughing and drinking and eating and whispering and, yes, even kissing in the quiet corners. We pass an elegant bar and enter a candlelit room filled with giant green ferns and black lacquer tables. We are seated at red velvet chairs, facing each other. Once settled, Nicole smiles at me from across the table and then asks if I like it here.

I nod. Yes, I like it here!

Nicole explains that we will simply have an *apéro*—a glass of wine—here at Hôtel Particulier, and then for dinner, she will take me to La Mascotte.

"I know all the secret places in Paris," she says in a low voice. *"Not typical tourist things. Special things. Authentique."* Nicole tells me about her company, called Personal Paris, and her website dedicated to custom-made tours, VIP services, and events. She creates Paris experiences for her clients and shows them the real Paris that only a local really knows. *"In Paris,"* she explains, *"you need a code."* Then she lowers her eyes and adds, *"I have the code."*

I love the way she says this, pursing her red-lipsticked lips and smiling slightly. But it's her voice that is the most disarming part of her charm. This is when I notice that while the restaurant is very crowded and I am surrounded by French people talking, I can't hear what they're saying. This is the key to the French voice. They never shout, but rather they lower their voices so that everything they say becomes even more intriguing.

I imagine that the couples are all having clandestine love affairs and whispering scandalous secrets to each other. They are probably not doing this, but still I do believe it's that hush-hush quality that makes the French voice so sexy.

OYSTERS, CHAMPAGNE, AND GIFTS FROM THE SEA

Later, Nicole takes me on another cobblestone walk down the hill and then over to Rue des Abbesses. I recognize the street from Woody Allen's *Midnight in Paris,* but I don't mention this, because I am so delighted when she takes me into La Mascotte, the brasserie. I look at all the seafood—oysters, scallops, prawns, and snails—displayed like beautiful works of art on piles of chipped ice. Nicole explains that this is where we will have dinner and that La Mascotte, originally opened in 1889, is famous for its seafood.

We toast with flutes of champagne, and oysters arrive shortly after that. And then Monsieur Campion, the owner of La Mascotte, arrives at our table. He is such a gentleman, dressed in a blue suit, with a salmon-toned tie, and he kisses Nicole on each cheek, *à la française,* and takes my hand, greeting me with so much warmth and charm.

MIDNIGHT IN PARIS

Nicole is telling me about her many visits to New York City and Cape Cod and how much she adores staying with her American friends in Greenwich Village's historic Patchin Place.

Somehow we are the last patrons at La Mascotte. The evening has just flown by, and now Nicole and I are getting ready to leave, but before this, Monsieur Campion returns to our table and he and Nicole exchange a few words. They are speaking softly in French, and somehow, before I know what is happening, Monsieur Campion gives me a gift—three cans of sardines. Nicole explains to me that these sardines are very special and very fine.

Each can has a picture of a French girl on the cover. My favorite is the one with the red-haired mermaid, wearing a blue dress made of shimmering fish scales.

Nicole explains that these sardines are from La Perle des Dieux in Saint-Gilles-Croix-de-Vie and that like French wine, they have all been stamped with a date and will only become more delicious as time goes by. They are good for ten years and, in fact, each can of sardines has won the prestigious Millésime award.

Honestly, I don't think I'll ever take sardines for granted again!

YOUR VOICE IS AN INSTRUMENT

Even if you don't have a French accent and you'll never be able to speak like my charismatic friend Nicole, nonetheless, you do have a voice, so why not recognize it as a powerful tool of seduction?

And just as important, consider not speaking. Think about the power of listening. In fact, if you speak a little less, then when you do speak up, men are more likely to pay attention. Think about your choice of words and the images you conjure with your language. Why not create a dreamy and beautiful painting with your words, modulating your tone and volume so it's almost a whisper? Talk about nature—the sky, clouds, flowers, and water. Describe a delicious meal—the flavors of lemon and rosemary, mint and tarragon. Talk about the feel of silk and satin, and the salty sea air on your skin when you visited the seashore last summer. You see how this works? When you engage in a little word painting, you can truly capture a man's imagination. You can then con-jure up people and places, all in the dream of your words. Never

Never forget how powerful your voice can be.

forget how powerful your voice can be. Take good care of it. Treasure it, because it is your magic flute.

Simply knowing this will change your life.

Parisian Charm School Lesson

The next time you watch a French film with subtitles, take a few minutes to close your eyes and just listen to the French voice. It's so sexy—even when the characters are talking or arguing about the most mundane things, such as how they've been wait-ing in that café for so long and their friend Marie-Claire is late, *as usual*. It's all so enticing—and you could say, well, it's all those *shhhhing* and *ooooohing* sounds. *It's part of the French language.* It's all those soft consonants and round vowels.

SOFTEN YOUR VOICE, AND YOU'LL BEGIN TO SOFTEN YOUR HEART.

And while this is partly true, you'll notice that when you really listen to the French speak—especially French women—you can hear how they will use their voices as if they were fine musical instruments—sometimes going fast, then slow, coaxing, flirting, rolling their *R*s, and always including more than a hint of mystery.

Take a look at the quintessential French film *Amélie*, starring Audrey Tautou. There, you'll find the scene where she helps a blind man walk down the crowded boulevard, holding his arm, weaving in and out of foot traffic, and all the while describing the sights and sounds swirling around them— the smiling owner of the flower shop, the bakery with lollipops, the cheese shop, the sugarplum ice cream, and a man in front of the produce shop giving out free melon slices. All during this dizzying scene, Amélie speaks quickly in French, describing the delicious imagery of Paris. Her voice is musical, soft, and enticing and makes everything she has to say sound like a wonderful secret.

Yes, part of the reason the dialogue sounds so beautiful to our ears is simply the French language itself, but more than this, Amélie's (or Audrey Tautou's) voice is lovely because of the words she chooses and how she creates a sensory-rich experience for us, delighting in all the sights, sounds, and smells of a busy afternoon in Paris filled with joie de vivre.

Of course, there's also the subtlety in her delivery. She never raises her voice, so that she and the man share their secret delight. It's a completely captivating scene and you are swept away by it, just as the man in the street is swept away under the spell of her enchantment.

Americans have a reputation for loud voices. We laugh loudly.

We shout out our greetings and we tend to make ourselves heard whether we're in a crowded subway or a quiet restaurant. And the truth is, it leaves nothing to the imagination. And it's just not necessary to be so loud, plus it's not very sexy. As the old ad from French perfumier Coty so wisely said, *If you want to attract someone's attention, whisper.*

Parisian Charm School Pratique

Start by recording your voice and really listening to it. Ask yourself if it's possible to modulate your tone, to speak more softly and seductively.

Next, think about the words you choose. Are they pretty? Do they paint a delightful picture? Do you paint imagery in your conversation? If you swear a lot, consider toning it down. Subtlety can be so much more impactful than brute force.

Finally, be like French women and think of your voice as a gift you give to the world. If we don't shout, we encourage people to lean in and listen. And the words we choose are important because we are painting pictures with our language. Consider the power your voice holds and use it to make the world a more delightful place. After all, you never know who's listening. Perhaps love is right around the corner and your voice will be his very first impression.

CHAPTER NINE

Food Is Love:
The French Dinner Party

A new dress doesn't get you anywhere.
It's the life you're leading in the dress.
—DIANA VREELAND

YOU'VE PROBABLY HEARD OF THE FRENCH
madeleine. They're the butter "cookies" made with lemon zest and baked in scallop-shaped molds. They're brown and crispy on the outside and soft and spongy—and buttery—on the inside. They've certainly arrived in America. Martha Stewart has an excellent recipe for them, using hazelnuts, and these days you can even find them at Starbucks!

In France, madeleines are actually considered to be a tea cake. You may know Proust's famous madeleine, featured in his beloved and classic book *Remembrance of Things Past: Swann's Way.* You may recall the story of how the memories of the narrator's childhood suddenly resurface when he takes a taste of the madeleine, dipped in his Aunt's lime flower tea.

But here's what you might not know—in Proust's first draft of *Swann's Way*, it was not a madeleine that he dipped into his tea, but rather an ordinary piece of toast. Yes, the plebeian toast—so humble and unromantic, and not named after a mysterious French woman known as Madeleine. I'm not sure if the notion of a "Proustian memory" would be studied by psychologists and mentioned in *Scientific America* and find its way into popular culture if it had been a mere piece of toast.

That's the power of a cookie. Okay, a tea cake.

And it's also why no book on captivating a man's heart *à la française* would be complete without a discussion on the seduction of sharing a meal, a dessert, a glass of champagne, and a kiss (or two or three).

It's mid-October and I am wearing my favorite polka-dot dress and the navy jacket I bought in Toulouse. Despite the fact that the weather has turned chilly in Paris, I come upon thirty or forty men and women outside on the terrace, drinking, laughing, and flirting. They come from all over the world, and most of them have never met before in their lives, but here they are, gathered outside of Jim Haynes's Paris apartment in the 14th arrondissement.

The soirée is hosted by Jim Haynes, world citizen. Actually, he's a writer and a cultural provocateur originally from Louisiana, born in 1933.

This is my first time at the famous soirée, and I receive by e-mail explicit instructions: take the metro to Alesia, walk out to rue de la Tombe-Issoire, and walk "exactly thirty-nine steps." Once at the building, enter a secret code, push the gate open, and walk down a cobblestone path through a garden. This part is quite surprising. From outside, on the street, everything feels very urban—but once you're inside, it feels as if you're in a charming country village with small brick buildings and little gardens.

Jim will accept the first fifty to sixty people who ask for an invitation. You must e-mail asking for a reservation, and then he will give you the directions and the code once everything is confirmed. It's all worth it because Jim Haynes's soirées are a part of Parisian history. Some very famous people have come through his doors over the past thirty years, including Germaine Greer, Allen Ginsberg, Yoko Ono, and Chloë Sevigny. The apartment is just down the street from 18 Villa Seurat, where Henry Miller lived and wrote *Tropic of Cancer* in 1934, with financial backing from Anaïs Nin, who, along with her husband, paid the rent and financed the first printing of the book.

I pour myself a glass of cabernet and say hello to a few guests and then walk up the stairs in search of Jim. I find him right away. He's lying on the couch by the door, greeting everyone, but also resting. He's just returned from a trip to London, and he is eighty-three, after all. Despite that, he has a young and energetic aura about him. And with his slightly shaggy mop of gray hair and big mustache, along with the turtleneck sweater, he gives off a strong beatnik vibe. Certainly, he's been influenced by the beats, as you can see from his bookshelves and vast collection of literature. His latest release is *World Citizen at Home in Paris*.

Jim welcomes me so warmly, I feel as if we have known each for decades. He suggests I line up for dinner, which is a potluck cooked by a volunteer visitor from Barcelona who stands behind a long buffet table and dishes out stew from a large pot. I take my place at the end of the line with a group of friendly diners to my right and to my left. We are served a ladle of stew, and then couscous. Later, there is salad, then cheese, and finally, cake and coffee. Everything is served on china. No paper or plastic.

Once I have my plate, I walk into the room and I'm immediately swept into a whirlwind of international conversation. I meet three gentlemen—one from Australia, one from Ireland, and another one from France. We sit together with Edith, my Parisian friend, and we immediately get into a lively conversation about men and women and the future of romance. And I don't think this is because I happen to write about men and love and romance. I think it's the food, the wine, the lively mix of young and old, local and foreign. I think it's the casual, slightly chaotic feel of the evening. It's improvisational and so very alive with possibility.

WHY WAITING IN LINE IS GOOD FOR LOVE

Reflecting on that line where we all stood and waited for our stew, it's clear to me that chatting with the visiting cook from Barcelona was a very important part of this flirtatious experience. You might think this method of waiting in line asking the cook for more or less stew seems inefficient, but I believe that this is actually one of the most important elements to the success of Jim's soirée, because it slows down the line. That's right, it *slows down* the line! You must talk while you're waiting and there's opportunity to talk about how you really love couscous or how you'd like just one piece of bread. And later, when all those dishes need to be washed—well, I can tell you, it was very,

very festive, and I do believe the man from Barcelona may have just found the woman he will spend the rest of his life with—or at least the next three weeks!

A MOVEABLE FEAST

I think there's a myth that French dinner parties are very staid and formal and fraught with political and cultural intrigue where if you don't sound very, very clever and witty and know how to drop more than a few *bon mots*, well, then it's off to the guillotine with you!

In fact, many French dinner parties are very casual, and quite a few are not even held indoors.

My friends Freddie and Pierre go on the *BiBaCa,* which stands for *Biclou Baguette & Camembert* (Bicycle, Baguette, and Camembert). It's an annual bike ride through the ancient city of Rouen, just outside Paris. The idea of the festival originated in Paris, where they have Béret Baguette. Freddie's friend Thierry wanted to have something like this for their friends in Normandy (that's why one of the specialities of the region, camembert, was added to the name). This is an annual September event in which everyone gets dressed in vintage clothing and wears worker's caps or straw boaters or berets, and often striped Breton tops with red scarves tied around the neck. The men will often wear suspenders, and the women seem to favor polka dots. And, of course, at the end of the bike trip, there's music and partner dancing and food.

To begin the day, about thirty men and women meet up in the city center and then go by bike to the countryside, where they enjoy a picnic lunch on tables in a field on the banks of the

River Seine in Rouen. Everyone brings something to share—wine or bubbly water; baguettes; camembert and other regional cheeses such gruyere, fromage de chévre, Roquefort; and delicatessen items, such as saucisson, andouille, ham, and rillette; as well as tomatoes, fruits, and, of course, French red wine and cider. People bring fruit and dessert. Inevitably, someone brings along an accordion or a guitar, and so the festivities include singing. The trip was originally organized to celebrate 1936, the year that employees were given two-week paid leave in France. The holiday is also a way for the French people to thank their grandparents, who fought so hard to win this freedom that the French still enjoy today.

Honestly, I can't think of a more delightful way to celebrate one's freedom. This is the perfect combination of food, fun, nature, exercise, fresh air, conversation, and music and a recipe for true romance.

ROMANCING THE HOME

When I asked my friend Valerie about how to create a seductive dinner at home, she explained to me that everything must be romantic, including the table setting. She suggests using a white tablecloth, but then your dress, makeup, and nail polish should be in harmony with your dishes. And of course, you'll want to have flowers or even branches or leaves that go with your table setting, depending on the season. Here's what she told me:

> *"For a night of romance without a lot of headache, it's important to prepare most everything in advance because you don't want to spend too much time in the kitchen.*

"Begin with champagne, then serve a little appetizer, such as foie gras on toasted bread, but paté is a nice substitute, and if you want to keep it light, just serve some olives and perhaps cherry tomatoes. It's important to keep your dinner light, because if you make something too heavy, you'll both be asleep before you're ready for any sort of dessert. And so, fish is always a good idea. Also, be careful with overdoing spices."

Just as an aside, I love the salads I've had in France where they'll take goat cheese and cut it into the shape of a heart and then place it in a little bed of green salad, and finally add some drops of fig flavor onto the cheese. It's so yummy. If you can't find fig flavor, then use real figs or some really good fig or raspberry jam.

"For dessert, enjoy an espresso and a compote of apple that you've prepared ahead of time, and then add a little spoonful of honey and Armagnac. Oh, and you might also enjoy a little glass of Armagnac."

KITCHEN ESSENTIALS

Of course, when you don't live in France some of this might not be possible to replicate, so you should make the offerings—and the evening—your own. The point is to always have a few things ready and to make the menu as easy and simple as possible. One way to do this is to keep your kitchen stocked with essentials. When I asked my French friends what they keep in their cupboards and fridges, they came up with some great suggestions, and I list them here (in no particular order):

Champagne

Can of sardines

Olive oil

Balsamic vinegar or wine vinegar

Onions

Garlic

Shallots

Paté

Eggs

Pasta

Butter

Olives

Parmesan cheese and one other cheese you really love

Good coffee

Milk

Crème fraîche (fresh cream)

Plain yogurt

Dark chocolate *(practically every single French person I asked said they couldn't live without chocolate)*

Dry white wine

Sweet white wine

Red wine (Bordeaux and Burgundy)

Bread*

Bowl of fruit on table

Spices, baking powder, herbs (especially thyme and bay leaf)

Herbal tea

Mineral water

Lemons

Fresh flowers (not to eat, but essential for joie de vivre)

---

*If you have a day to prepare, I suggest you make Jim Lahey's no-knead bread recipe from his book *My Bread: The Revolutionary No-Work, No-Knead Method*. All you need on hand is all-purpose flour, instant yeast, salt, and a little corn meal or wheat bran. It's almost like having a Parisian *boulangerie* in your own kitchen.

FRENCH MEN COOK

Pierre is married to Freddie. They're the couple that went on the yearlong world tour. At home, Pierre does most of the cooking because he has a real passion for gastronomy. He comes from the southwest of France, the heart of *gastronomique*. He learned to cook with his mother when he was quite young and always hungry. So his love of cooking comes from that. He tells me that for him, cooking is a kind of meditation. And since he's traveled to so many countries around the world, he's gone beyond the traditional French ingredients and likes to include products such as fresh ginger, fresh coriander, cumin, curry, sumac, cardamom, turmeric, and nutmeg in his culinary creations.

Pierre was kind enough to give me this recipe for daube, or beef stew, saying that it's perfect for dinner parties because you can prepare it the day before. On the day of the party you can spend time with your friends, instead of being in the kitchen, doing the cooking. The daube creates a wonderful conviviality and it's especially great during the winter, when it's cold outside and everyone wants to come inside and get warm. Pierre tells me that the daube is a magic dish because the more it's reheated, the better it gets, and it can be kept in the fridge for at least four or five days. The daube is eaten with potatoes served, as the French say, in *robe des champs*. The literal translation is "dress that you wear in the fields" and basically means that you serve the daube with small, unpeeled potatoes.

Serve a good Bordeaux or Burgundy with your daube.

DAUBE FROM PIERRE DUBERNET
(BEEF BOURGUIGNON)

INGREDIENTS

4 lbs, 6 ounces of beef to
be braised (chuck) cut
into large cubes

6 tablespoons olive oil

1 ¾ ounces flour

2 tomatoes

4 garlic cloves

1 teaspoon tomato paste

1 bouquet garni (mixed
herbs)

salt and pepper

3 cups full-bodied red
wine (Cahors type)

grated nutmeg

10 ½ ounces small
onions

1 ounce butter

1 teaspoon sugar

2 tablespoons water

7 ounces smoked bacon

1 bunch flat parsley

pasta or polenta
(optional)

1. Wash, dry, and cut the tomatoes into pieces. Peel and crush the garlic cloves.

2. Heat 4 tablespoons of oil in a large casserole. Brown the meat cubes on all sides. Reduce the flame and mix in the flour with the meat cubes so that they are well coated.

3. Add tomatoes, garlic, tomato paste, bouquet garni, a few peppercorns, and salt. Pour the wine and mix well while bringing to a boil. Skim off fat. Cover and let simmer over very low heat for 4 hours. Add a little grated nutmeg.

4. Peel the onions and put them in a saucepan with butter, sugar, and 2 tablespoons of water. Let simmer over very low heat, covered, until the onions are tender and a little caramelized.

5. As the onions are cooking, cut the bacon into large pieces and sauté them in a frying pan with the remaining oil. Add them to the casserole, with the onions, 15 minutes before the end of the cooking of the stew. Sprinkle with chopped parsley and serve with pasta or polenta.

THE FRENCH GIRL AND THE AMERICAN GI

My friend Alexandra's French mother, Pierrette, passed away recently at the age of eighty-nine. She was a wonderful cook, and Alexandra told me the story of how her mother came to America:

"My mother was born in 1927 in north Algeria. My grandparents owned a café, Le Café de Cadix, where she worked as a barmaid. She met my father, John, when she was seventeen years old. This was during World War II and he was an American GI stationed in her town. He often came into their café.

"He immediately fell in love with my mother, and apparently, he asked her to marry him a couple of times, but she refused; and then on Christmas Eve he came to the café with gifts for everyone, including the housekeeper. My mother didn't have a gift for him, so as the story goes she decided to give him her hand in marriage as a gift!

"*She came to the States as a war bride, not speaking any English. She told us that she taught herself to read by listening to American soap operas on the radio. She went on to raise six children. I was lucky enough to live with my parents overseas for over ten years during my childhood when they retired abroad. She loved to cook, entertain, and make clothes from scratch because they couldn't always afford the finer things. She absolutely loved decorating houses. In her last years, because she couldn't hear very well, Facebook became the center of her world so that she could stay in touch with everyone and write and communicate with friends and family.*

> ## 'There's nothing that can't be fixed with a little garlic and parsley.'

"*I remember, she used to say 'the hat or the hair,' meaning pick one thing, you can't have the fancy hat and the wild hair, but she would apply that to most clothing and outfits in general—meaning nothing* de trop *(too much.) Until her dying breath, her favorite song was Gloria Gaynor's* I Will Survive. *She always said, 'There's nothing that can't be fixed with a little garlic and parsley.'*

"*Paella was her* specialité du maison *(her speciality of the house), and she actually bought all six of her children their own paella pans, years ago.*

"*Everything she made tasted so good because as she would always say, 'it was cooked with love.'*"

Here is Alexandra's mother's recipe for paella, the *specialité du maison*, to you, with love:

1 cup chopped fresh
   parsley

¼ cup fresh lemon juice

1 tablespoon olive oil

2 large garlic cloves,
   minced

Paella:

1 cup water

1 teaspoon saffron
   threads

2 cups chicken
   broth

8 unpeeled jumbo shrimp

olive oil (as needed)

4 skinless, boneless chicken
   thighs, cut in half

4 links Spanish chorizo
   sausage (about 6 ½
   ounces)

2 cups finely chopped
   onion

1 cup finely chopped red
   bell pepper

1 cup canned diced
   tomatoes, undrained

1 teaspoon sweet paprika

3 large garlic cloves,
   minced

3 cups uncooked yellow,
   Arborio, or other
   short-grain rice

1 cup frozen green peas

8 mussels, scrubbed and
   debearded

¼ cup fresh lemon juice

Lemon wedges

Combine the first 4 ingredients and set aside.

To prepare the paella, combine the water, saffron, and broth in a large saucepan. Bring to a simmer (do not boil). Keep warm over low heat. Peel and devein shrimp, leaving tails intact; set aside.

Heat 1 tablespoon oil in a large paella pan or large skillet over medium-high heat. Add chicken; sauté 2 minutes on each side. Remove from pan. Add sausage; sauté 2 minutes. Remove from pan. Add shrimp; sauté 2 minutes. Remove from pan. Reduce heat to medium-low. Add onion and bell pepper; sauté 15 minutes, stirring occasionally. Add tomatoes, paprika, and garlic cloves; cook 5 minutes. Add rice; cook 1 minute, stirring constantly. Stir in herb blend, broth mixture, chicken, sausage mixture, and peas. Bring to a low boil; cook 10 minutes, stirring frequently. Add mussels to pan, nestling them into rice mixture. Cook 5 minutes or until shells open; discard any unopened shells. Arrange shrimp, heads down, in rice mixture, and cook 5 minutes or until shrimp are done. Sprinkle with ¼ cup lemon juice. Remove from heat; cover with a towel, and let stand 10 minutes. Serve with lemon wedges, if desired.

MASTER ONE GREAT DISH AND MAKE IT YOUR SPECIALITÉ DU MAISON.

FIONA'S BIRTHDAY CAKE

Everyone in France seems to know and love this very simple cake recipe. It's been written up in lots of books, and in fact, I included my friend's version of it with crunchy lemon icing in my second book, *Bonjour, Happiness!* I enjoyed it most recently while in Saclas with Kate. She served it for her daughter's birthday and spread it with raspberry jam and placed a little edible flower on top. It was really charming. She gave me the recipe in French, explaining that the French refer to it as one-pot yogurt cake because you use those little yogurt pots to measure most of the ingredients. Clever, *non?*

RECETTE DU GÂTEAU AU YAOURT
(RECIPE FOR YOGURT CAKE)

Preheat oven to 350 degrees.

Grease and line one round cake pan.

Mix dry ingredients first, then add wet ingredients:

1 pot sugar (½ cup)
4 pots flour (2 cups)

2 ¼ teaspoon baking powder

Mix and then stir in:

2 pots of yogurt (or 1 cup)
3 eggs

1 pot vegetable oil (½ cup)
Zest of ½ unwaxed lemon

Whisk well with a wooden spoon.

Bake for 40 minutes, or until a knife comes out clean.

Cool and sprinkle with confectioner's sugar.

Layer with your choice of jam. (We use our homemade wild raspberry jam, but I know some French who use apricot jam and it's very good!)

Enjoy!

I am not claiming that you'll get slim enjoying all these delectable dishes, but I do believe that they will pave the way for romance and love, friendship, kinship, and general good feelings. Don't be afraid of food! It's important to indulge your senses, because when you do you will find that good food, prepared with love and respect, will sustain body and soul.

French women know this, and we do, too, although sometimes I think in the interest of watching our waistlines, we've sacrificed one of our most charming tools we possess in our arsenal—food and its power to seduce, disarm, and simply put everyone in a good mood. Every meal is an opportunity to gather and celebrate and even flirt and fall in love.

Parisian Charm School Lesson

In France, I think more men have a love of cooking than women—and that's because they know from experience that it leads to romance!

And isn't it so much more romantic than a date in a restaurant? The fact is, French women don't date very much. They simply don't see the point in going out on the one-on-one interview-style meet-up at a pricey restaurant and then sitting across from a virtual stranger and trying to find out who he really is, how she feels about him, and whether there's actually a possibility for a future together—all in two to three hours.

However, French women *will* meet men at dinner parties. And even when it's clear there's a romantic spark, French women still don't date, but rather they will go for a walk or meet in the park and enjoy a casual picnic.

Dinner parties are the perfect subterfuge for meeting a new man, but they're also the perfect opportunity for seeing an interesting man over the course of many days and nights, in a variety of venues and combination of people.

At a dinner party, you can witness how a man interacts with male friends, with other women, with children, with the elderly, and with family.

This is because French dinner parties are intergenerational and there's a constant influx of new people to keep things lively and interesting. While many American women are intimidated by the idea of hosting a dinner party, it's important to understand that these dinner parties are often rather casual, last-minute affairs where a homemade soup (prepared ahead of time, over the weekend) is paired with a nice salad, bread, and a dessert bought at the local bakery. Oftentimes, the dinner party is a potluck, and in those tiny French apartments, it's okay to sit on the floor.

French women meet men in groups, rather than alone. This way, there's lots of time and many opportunities to get to know a man in the context of friends and family. There's absolutely no pressure to take the relationship from friendship to romance quickly. These get-togethers give women lots of opportunities to practice the art of charm, to hone their flirtation skills and to gain confidence. These dinner parties provide a kind of "charm school" for French women and while there might be some missteps when she first begins attending parties (although young girls in France are usually included in parties), over time, her sense of self-possession and élan grows.

Parisian Charm School Pratique

Even if you've never hosted a dinner party before, it's never too late to hone your skills. Start small by meeting up with a group of friends at a local bistro, bar, or restaurant. Expand your core group to include interesting men. These are "practice" encounters, and it's actually best not to include a man you're secretly in love with at the beginning, but rather a fun male friend.

Create a monthly potluck get-together, ever-expanding the core group. Consider what activities could be the unifying purpose for the gatherings. Picnics in the park are always a good idea, and this is especially true if there's music and dancing. Spread your wings and see what develops. Sharing stories and laughter with friends new and old—what could be more charming than that?

CHAPTER TEN

Mistresses, Marriage, and Mystery

Whoever has loved,
knows all that life contains of sorrow and joy.
—GEORGE SAND

I OFTEN THINK ABOUT THAT OLD DIXIE CUPS song "Going to the Chapel of Love." The lyrics are all about going to the chapel, getting married—and most important, the idea that "we'll love until the end of time and we'll never be lonely anymore."

It's true, we all want to feel safe. We want reassurances that we will love and be loved and that nothing will ever interfere with this moment and that everything will always stay exactly the same. Perfect. Forever.

But we all know that nothing stays the same. Life changes. People change.

People leave you. People you thought you'd never see again,

suddenly return. People surprise you in the most unexpected way. Life brings you great joy, but life also brings with it great sadness, even tragedy and loss.

Honestly, I am a mere child compared to my French sisters. I simply assume I am entitled to life, liberty, and the pursuit of happiness. I take for granted there will be love and joy and delicious meals and romantic nights by the fireplace with Dr. Thompson. Perhaps I don't assume, as in the song, that now that I've gone to "the chapel of love" I will never be lonely anymore, but you know what? Maybe deep down, I do.

French women most definitely do not make these assumptions. Ever. They're a whole lot more existential about life and love, and they also seem to live in the present a whole lot more than the rest of us do.

THE MUSEUM OF LOST THINGS

I do believe that this existentialism comes out of a history of countless invasions over the years into the tiny country of France and, in particular, their experiences during World War I—or as it was known at the time, the Great War, also called the War to End All Wars (only it didn't).

My good friend Margie moved to France over thirty years ago and lives in the city of Lille. Before moving to Lille, she lived in Morbecque, a little village on the border of Belgium and France. I visited her home about ten years ago and she suggested we drive over to Belgium and visit In Flanders Fields, the World War I museum in the ancient town of Ypres.

We entered the museum and began our tour by first selecting a card from a box. This card was my "person," and the idea was that we would go through the chronology of the war—the invasion of France and Belgium by the Germans, the trenches, the arrival of the British, the Australians—and see the events through different people's points of view.

I got the card with a picture of a thirty-seven-year-old French woman who owned a hat shop in a little village outside of Paris. I held on to her card as if it were some kind of talisman, hoping she would survive. As Margie and I circled around the displays of gas masks and red and blue uniforms, photographs and letters, I kept looking at her face—her dark eyes with her serious expression and pursed lips. I hoped that she would make it through to the end of the war. And then maybe I would find out whether she was still alive today. That would have made her nearly one hundred years old at the time of our visit, but you never know.

Truthfully, the tour was rough. There were some heart-wrenching photographs of young men in cornflower-blue uniforms marching off to war from all over France and Belgium—from the cities and the villages—only to find themselves dying terrible deaths in trenches filled with frozen mud.

This was during the advent of chemical warfare, so there was mustard gas that pretty much guaranteed a horrific death, and if you survived, you were left disfigured for life. Back in Paris, the government rationed bread and coal and grain—this during one of the coldest winters on record. And then there was the Spanish influenza, killing 1,778 civilians in one week.

And when it was all over, France lost almost 5 percent of its entire population, leaving behind a devastated and traumatized country. Those who survived would become known as the Lost Generation.

And my French shop lady? Well, I left the shadows of the

World War I exhibition and entered the sunlit room of the gift shop, I opened up my envelope to find that, no, she did not survive the war.

IN FLANDERS FIELD, A POPPY GROWS

If she had survived, she would find herself living in a country where there were simply not enough men to go around. In addition to this unhappy development, the men who actually did survive the war were often disfigured and maimed, and literally as well as psychically scarred beyond repair. In fact, over half the men died or were maimed. Madame M. still remembers the streets of Paris being filled with such men, legless, rolling about on wooden pallets. This was before prosthetics and plastic surgery.

France became a country with limited food resources, filled with widows and orphans. Marrying and starting a family was simply not possible. This is one of the underlying reasons why the French may be a little less judgmental when it comes to the role of the mistress in their society.

So what did French women—many of them young widows with children—do after the trauma of war, surrounded by crippled men and orphans? Well, they didn't crumble and fold. They put on a brave face. They mended their old dresses. They put newspaper in the soles of their worn shoes. They got creative with a bit of lace or a new set of buttons. They brushed their hair and put on a bit of lipstick. They developed gifts that cost nothing—the art of clever conversation, dancing, and, most assuredly, charm, because charm will go a long, long way in the land of loss.

LEARN TO ENJOY SIMPLE PLEASURES THAT COST NOTHING AT ALL.

And with only these things at their disposal, the women of France got to work. They got creative.

A FLOWER IN HER LAPEL

One such woman was Madame Anna Guérin, a French teacher who traveled extensively during and after the war giving talks and raising awareness. She created the "Remembrance Poppy Day." She organized French widows and orphans to make cloth poppies to be pinned on one's lapel and sold them on her tours during poppy drives, with the proceeds going to help World War I invalids and their widows and orphans. We still have them today and while you don't see these so much anymore in America, on November eleventh, Armistice Day, practically everyone in Great Britain,

Australia, and Canada wears a red "Remembrance Poppy" on their lapel. The French will wear a blue cornflower, known as *Le Bleuet de France,* to match the French uniforms during the Great War, to commemorate their loved ones they lost during those terrible years.

Today, we see this idea of wearing a pretty flower pin on your lapel. Whenever we wear a pink ribbon to support breast cancer research or to honor our fallen sisters, we must know that we are part of a grand tradition of women who take a little bit of ribbon or cotton or silk and turn it into something powerful and charming.

FLOWERS ON THE MANTELPIECE

For French women the idea of survival lives on beyond the blue cornflower or the red poppy on the lapel. The legacy lives on in a kind of psychic cultural shift that can be seen in their attitudes toward marriage and guarantees. And so, even getting married is not as important to the French as it is to Americans. They simply don't believe in guarantees, and they know for certain that even if they go to the "chapel of love," they will more than likely still find themselves lonely at times.

And perhaps, too, they will turn a blind eye to their husband's dalliances, because it has only been a few generations since they lost the luxury of complete candor and righteous honesty. They just don't have the heart to hold a man's feet to the fire over infidelity. Yes, they forgive and forget some of the details and move on to the important bigger picture of life.

Through years of hardship and uncertainty, French women have developed a way to take care of the glue that keeps the fabric of society together—a handmade dress that's been repeatedly repaired and well pressed, shoes that may have been reheeled and reheeled again, and pretty lingerie that lasts a long, long time because it's been lovingly washed by hand. The French woman shows her love and gratitude with a simple but whole-some meal, a humble bouquet of wildflowers placed above the fire on the mantelpiece, a kiss for her husband, her partner, or her lover and a timeless set of rules for her children that have kept her world together and tied the past to the present, with the comforting knowledge that despite the unpredictable nature of life, certain things will never change.

> ## APPRECIATE THE HERE AND NOW, KNOWING THAT EVERYTHING COULD CHANGE TOMORROW.

French women know that the world can go insane tomorrow and we can lose everything, but we have an unspoken agree-ment that we will put love above all else and we will live in the gray area—that mysterious place where uncertainty resides and forgiveness blooms.

Parisian Charm School Lesson

The French simply do not have the same kind of illusions about the big white wedding dress and the happily ever after. I've come to understand that some of their rationality and pragmatism toward the institution of marriage derives from their own tumultuous past.

This is not to say that in today's France, infidelity is completely accepted. In fact, many French women have told me that if their husband were to stray, it would be the end of the marriage.

Nonetheless, the reality is that the French are not always faithful. But guess what—Americans aren't always faithful, either! And so, knowing this, it's up to us to take nothing for granted and to do our very best to create a beautiful life full of romance, mystery, and charm. There are no guarantees in life, so why not seize the day and express love now, in small, ordinary, everyday ways?

Take a cue from our French sisters and develop your inner strengths, knowing that ultimately, we must be self-reliant. Look for simple moments of joie de vivre—joy in living—knowing that the future is now.

Appreciate the mystery hidden inside your own love affair or marriage.

Living in the moment, the "French woman way" means finding everyday happiness, making home-cooked meals, using our good silverware every day, and bringing nature into our homes. Appreciate the mystery hidden inside your own love affair or marriage, not seeking any guarantees, but embracing the unknown. This is truly "the sweet spot"—that place in a relationship where you look at your lover or husband and you realize that you don't truly know him. And he doesn't truly know you, and this is what keeps your love story alive and growing and beautiful.

Parisian Charm School Pratique

Consider how we can live better with less. Clear out the excess in your closets and cupboards, so you might rediscover lovely things you've put away for "a rainy day." Once you've rediscovered those lovely things, be sure to use them often.

> **EMBRACE THE IDEA**
> **THAT LESS IS MORE.**

Make your husband or boyfriend something delicious to eat. Take out your good silver and begin using it every day.

Forgive little transgressions and wear a flower in your lapel.

CHAPTER ELEVEN

How to Charm Your Husband

Let us be grateful to people who make us happy. They are the
charming gardeners who make our souls blossom.
—MARCEL PROUST

I AM ON THE TRAIN, THE TGV, TRAVELING FROM
Agen north to Paris. It's a little after noon, and I notice how all
my fellow passengers have left their seats. I realize I'm hungry,
and so I find my way to the dining car, and there I find a line
full of French people talking and gesturing. There is a part of
me—the American part of me—that thinks, *Oh, maybe I should
come back later when it's less crowded.* But then, I don't want to
miss this French scene. And it is a scene. The guy behind the
counter is laughing and joking with everyone, and the mood is
truly festive.

When it's finally my turn, I begin ordering in hesitant French
and he tells me, in really good English, that he lived in New
Orleans for many years and he speaks fluent English. *Small*

world, is all I can think. We have a lovely exchange about the jazz festival, Café Du Monde, beignets, and if I'd like something to drink with my little Caesar salad. No one in the line seems to mind the fact that the little conversation holds up the business of ordering lunch for a tiny bit. In fact, a man to my right seems to forget all about his lunch and wants to practice his English with us.

Once I have my salad, I have the choice to bring my tray back to my seat, which is only one car away, or to stay in the dining car and sit on a little stool by one of the crowded counters. Of course, I choose to stay. This is where it's all happening, after all.

Now, truthfully, the salad is nothing special. It's nice enough. And I do love the little bottles of oil and vinegar. There is a certain charm to this, but again, nothing to write home about. What is delightful is the sense of camaraderie among my dinner partners and the elegance of being in public and eating lunch with a group, even though I am actually dining alone.

I think there is something in our American sensibility that actually likes eating alone. I'm not sure what it is, but I see people going through the McDonald's drive-through at three in the afternoon. It is not lunchtime or dinnertime. But maybe that's the appeal—that fierce independence that says, *I'm free! I can eat a meal any time I feel like it!* Plus, there's the car and the drive-through. The only ones who will know what you're up to (extra-large chocolate milk shake?) are you and your maker. (The maker of the chocolate milk shake, that is. Not your *maker*.)

PRIVATE LIVES

In America, it would seem, we have made the public private and the private public. We wear our sweats and sometimes even our pajamas to the supermarket. We dine alone or in the car or in a dark room in front of the blue light of the television. Oh, and sometimes we wear our lingerie in public.

I actually have no objection to the last part—wearing lingerie in public—as long as it's a fashion statement and layered with something elegant, such as a smoking jacket. French women know that we need that important balance between sexy and classic and public and private.

This applies not simply to how we dress and dine, but also to how we fan the flames of our marriage or love affair. We must create and keep a clear delineation between what happens in public and what happens in private. French women are brilliant at maintaining a certain separateness and dignity, even in their private lives. They will wear pretty silk pajamas at home. Many French women have a separate dressing room/bath area. They do not ever "let themselves go," but rather they will hold themselves in and maintain an air of mystery. French women know that this is not only the way to charm, it's also how we can keep the tension in our romance.

Yes, tension. This notion of keeping tension in your relationship might make you feel anxious on the surface, but the truth is, tension comes from uncertainty, and uncertainty is actually your friend when it comes to yearning and desire. The truth is, too much closeness and familiarity with your partner is actually not good for your marriage. Your man is with you because you intrigued him. He wanted to get to know you better. And now, just because you are together doesn't mean the intrigue should stop. Both you and your man are constantly evolving. And this is what keeps your romance alive—this sense of the unknown.

CREATING RITUALS

Not too long ago, my new friend Marine from Duvelleroy in Paris told me a little secret about how French women keep their men intrigued throughout the years. She explained how we can create certain associations in our men's imagination. For example, when your man goes to a coat closet to fetch your coat, he will find himself inhaling the fragrance of your perfume on your scarf. Or, whenever he sees your signature color, whether it's blue or green or pink or orange, he will think of you. Even simple gestures like the click-click-click of your heels on pavement will make him think of you. You see, men are sensory creatures, and so everything you do and all your little routines and special signifiers are creating memories and mysteries that hold his intrigue.

This is the power of the tender push and pull between the familiar and the strange, the known and the unknown, the public and the private. Still, it's a dichotomy, because on one hand, we need to maintain mystery, and on the other hand, we need to create delicious associations. But here's another way to think about it: your man is hungry, and he can smell that roast in the oven, mysteriously simmering. He'd love to open the door, but truthfully, it's in both of your best interests not to let him take a taste until the roast is fully cooked and ready and his appetite has grown to the peak point of desire.

I'll go a little further with the metaphor. The roast is familiar and warm and pleasing, but the waiting and the not-knowing is the mystery. The appetite and the yearning for a taste is the tension. You need all three ingredients—mystery, yearning, and the familiar—to keep the love strong in your marriage.

MARRIAGE: CHARM SCHOOL
FOR ADVANCED LEARNERS

It's not always easy to maintain separateness and mystery. Inevitably, through the years, a certain amount of tension will disappear. And then the fact that marriage is a promise, a commitment, can create a little challenge in keeping romance from feeling like a *cage d'amour*. Yes, the promise of love is both wonderful and a little challenging. We don't want a love affair to devolve into a kind of casual sibling-style relationship, and yet we want our love and trust and deep and abiding friendship to grow over the course of many years—even while knowing that there are no guarantees in life.

How do French women do this? It's really very simple. French women go out into the world. They do not succumb to the lure of online shopping (at least not as much as many Americans), but rather they will walk to the market and the *boulangerie* on a daily basis. They will stop and talk to friends and neighbors along the way. They participate in local festivals and community activities. They will participate in the theater of life and "make a showing" on a daily basis.

Remember Nancy? She's my Estée Lauder friend who has been living in Paris for the past thirty years. She recently told me about her experiences watching her two daughters in the park on Saturdays. *"It's Saturday,"* she explains, *"and the women have their make-up on and are even better dressed than they are during the work week—if that's possible!"*

In France, there's no Casual Friday or even a Casual Saturday, and this is because dressing well is not only pleasurable for the one wearing something pretty, but also for anyone who is watching from the sidelines in the parks or in the café. Dressing well is a way to add some wind to your sails and certainly your man will take notice when you return home with an air of mystery, having left an unknowable amount of desire in your wake.

EVEN THE FURNITURE IS FLIRTING WITH YOU

It is springtime in Paris, and everywhere I look I see tassels. I think I've become obsessed with tassels. I find them on earrings, key chains, on the backs of shoes, and most of all—on the French furniture. The tassels come in all different sizes and colors. Some are aqua blue and some are hot pink. I keep seeing beautiful old French chairs with gold tassels and blooming with little rosettes and the most intricate embroidered trimmings. I ask Beatrice about this, and she nods at me with a knowing expression and whispers *"Ah, this is* passementerie. *It's very French."* I would love to come home from Paris with a tasseled chair, but since I really can't—at least not on this trip—instead I buy a souvenir hot pink tasseled key chain. On La Belle Farm, we still have the original 1820 skeleton key, and so I attach it to the key chain and place it in the door as a decoration.

This might sound completely incongruous—a hot pink tasseled key chain on an early American door—but it's not.

Honestly, it goes with the house. And it's sexy. Besides the two hot pink faux–Louis XVI chairs, that's the only hot pink in the house. Honest!

The point is, even your home can be a place that subtly (or perhaps not-so-subtly) conspires to keep your romance alive and well. Your home is a kind of theater set for your play. You might ask yourself—do I want to stage a comedy, a drama, or a romantic romp? It's up to you.

This is why French women will be careful not to let their common rooms become overrun with the trappings and responsibilities of domestic life. The children's toys are not a source of constant clutter. In fact, the French just do not accumulate a whole lot of stuff. You'll find that the principle of "less is more" is not only the way to a happy home, but it's also the route to romance. Rather than adding "stuff" to your married life, add experiential pleasures, such as beautiful music, excellent wine, and good food. Light candles. Make it a daily practice to watch the sunset together. Dress beautifully for each other. It's important that there is a place for

Create a space that is just for romance, just for the two of you.

you and your husband to be with each other without the responsibilities of day-to-day life—the bills to be paid, the plumbing to be repaired, and the errands to be run. Rather, create a space that is just for romance, just for the two of you.

BUILDING MEMORIES

Traveling by plane always makes for a long day. I began my morning in Paris, taking a taxi to Charles DeGaulle, waiting in countless lines, walking through long and crowded corridors, getting through security, stopping to shop in duty-free, and waiting in another line to board my flight, after which I'm in the air for six hours, cramped into a little window seat next to a six-foot-something businessman. And then, I arrive at Boston's Logan Airport and wait in some more lines where I slowly move forward, snaking around the cordons at customs, whereupon I take the elevator to baggage claim, and I wait in yet one more line, and then finally I am gloriously released into the arrivals room, where I look around at the crowd of waiting family and friends to find a handsome man in suit and tie, wearing sunglasses and, just like a professional limo driver, holding up a sign that says CALLAN.

That would be me.

Oh, and the handsome man is carrying a big bouquet of roses. This is the man I call Dr. Thompson. I call him *Dr. Thompson* because in the course of our romance he went from being my student in a writing class at Fairfield University to graduating from Columbia University, where he earned a PhD in geology, and then went on to become a scientist at Woods Hole Oceanographic Institution on Cape Cod, where we lived for ten years.

He's now retired and we live on a little farm in upstate New York, where he raises chickens and turkeys, tends to our apple orchard, grows amazing vegetables, and shows up at our local farmer's market every Sunday. I should probably call him "Farmer Bill," but truthfully, I love calling him Dr. Thompson. And this is because it adds a certain formality to our relationship.

I believe that maintaining a certain formality—in addition to rituals and elegance and apple pie—are the cornerstones to marriage.

LIVING IN A STATE OF WONDER

Irene Goodman has been my literary agent for over ten years, and I consider her a good friend and a great inspiration. She told me the most wonderful story the other day. She was in the country with her husband of many years when there was a big snowstorm. She looked out the window and told him in a wistful tone that she had never had a snowman as a child, but always wanted one. She suggested that they both go outside and make a snowman. Her husband said, "Maybe later."

Irene didn't think about this again, until the very next day, when her husband took her to the window and, holding her hand, pointed. There, on the deck, was the most perfect snowman, just for her. What a lovely surprise and what a wonderful way to show his love for her.

Still, it's important to note that she was not disappointed when her husband said, "Maybe later," but rather she was able to just be in that place between yearning and fulfillment. This is the place in a marriage where there are no guarantees. There is a slight loss of communication, something Dr. Phil might not approve of, but French women know this is the very stuff that keeps a marriage alive and growing and full of wonder.

WALK SOFTLY AND CARRY
A BIG BAG OF ORANGES

My dear friend Kelly came to Paris with me and a group of wonderful women for the 2014 *Ooh La La! Paris Tour*. I adored having her with us because she is a great observer of human behavior, she loves all things feminine, and she has an endless fascination for all things French. She's just a bit younger than I am and newly remarried. She's particularly interested in keeping her marriage spicy. After the tour ended, Kelly stayed on and rented an apartment for a week, so that she could experience Paris as a native—shopping, cooking, and wandering the streets on her own. I loved the story she told me upon her return from the City of Light.

> *"I was walking around the tenth arrondissement, wearing a new summer dress and lugging a bag of oranges. I saw a handsome young man coming my way, and I ducked my head a bit, in order to NOT make eye contact. But he greeted me very deliberately, as in 'Bonjoooooour, Madame!' and I yanked my chin up in time to catch a very flirty grin. He made me look. I thought, This flirting thing, it's a sport here, and I better get with the program!"*

And when she came home, this experience stayed with her, and she said yes, that in fact it rejuvenated her love affair with her husband.

> *"I always come back from Paris with a renewed vision of myself as a female. I remember, Ah yes, flirting! It really does put a bounce in my step! I sometimes forget how cheering and alluring that is for my husband. He smiles, he relaxes. Simple things, like my putting on a skirt to wear around the house, and turning a serious conversation with a little joke, changing the ions, and he responds. But I need reminding, all the time.*
>
> *"I'm operating in an almost macho, 'let's go!' energy a lot, and I forget how enervating that can be for him. Our culture prioritizes being on task and on time, even for children. Directness and time*

management outrank subtlety, or softness, or eye contact, or play-time. We lose the knack of our femininity. We forget to have fun!"

Ah, fun. Remember fun?

DON'T MONETIZE YOUR LOVE

I am in a shop on Rue de Bac. The handsome store clerk places my purchase in a bag and then takes my credit card. As he hands it back to me, he winks and asks, "And what's your phone number?"

I don't hesitate. I begin to give it to him. Okay, maybe for a moment I think it's a little strange, but I've become so conditioned by CVS and all those other stores that ask you for either your loyalty card or your phone number, that I've completely missed the fact that this dashing French man is flirting with me!

He asks me, rather teasingly, I might add, if I always give out my phone number so freely in America. I want to explain the bit about CVS, but honestly it seems too complicated, so I just say, no, I don't give out my phone number so freely, although the truth is, I think I do.

Leaving the shop, I wonder about this and how often my own culture elevates commerce over community, and whether or not in all this effort to make money or save money, we have sac-

Your romantic life is not a business.

rificed something very important to our own well-being. Have we sacrificed charm?

Perhaps it's time to take another look at our priorities and forgo expediency and efficiency for beauty, elegance, and the simple pleasures of life and love. Your romantic life is not a business. In fact, I would go so far as to say that the secret to keeping love alive is to forgo the mantras of capitalism—efficiency, expediency, time management, and all those lovely go-getter mantras. They are not the way to go when it comes to finding or keeping love. In fact, it's the opposite. It's when you are a *flâneur* (a person who strolls and explores their town or city) that you're more likely to find or rekindle your love. This is because love is waiting for you when you least expect it. Love happens when you're not looking. It's rekindled when you're not multitasking or saving money or "getting things done" or thinking about how to be more efficient.

> TAKE THE CIRCUITOUS ROUTE TO
> LOVE. IT'S MORE FUN AND MORE
> SURPRISING, AND MUCH SEXIER.

Well, there you have it—that's my two cents, and because the French don't measure things in cents, it's my *grain de sel,* my grain of salt.

Parisian Charm School Lesson

Love is creative. We are always creating our story. We are not "done" once we "get" the guy. No one gets to own anyone. We should take nothing for granted. We simply love and live and create our story. The dream is to make it a great one.

> *We are always creating our story.*

So even after the wedding and the honeymoon, even after the children leave for college, we must see our marriage as an ever-evolving story. We need to gain perspective and take a step back every now and then and look at our loved one from a distance, in a place where we can be observed as attractive to others. Husbands need to do this with their wives, and wives need to do this with their husbands. (By the way, this is another great reason to attend dinner parties.)

The French know that we all need to show our husbands and partners that we are still attractive to other men and that other men compliment us, even flirt with us. The French do not take this as an insult. In fact, a French man understands that when another man pays attention to his wife it's actually a compliment to him. His wife is clearly still worthy of *le regard*. The husband's ardor (whether their relationship is still in the courtship stage or they are facing the twilight years) can be renewed and refreshed in these moments.

We all need to be shaken up a little and reminded that life is not predictable and there are surprises and delights along the way and around every corner.

Embrace those spaces between yearning and desire, mystery and surprise. When we are in a marriage for a long time, we can lose this sense of mystery and we assume we know everything about our partner and he knows everything about us. And this may *seem* true, but it's really not. Human beings are never completely known. There is always mystery. It's simply a matter of identifying it and coaxing it to return to our everyday life.

Parisian Charm School Pratique

Bring a little romance into your own marriage by paying closer attention to what brings him joy, whether it means cooking his favorite dish or wearing a certain color that he loves. Talk to your husband about what you find appealing and romantic— not with any hidden agenda, but simply as a way to reconnect with him.

The French love to say *vive la différence*, which celebrates the differences between men and women. Try to not "collapse" into your marriage by becoming a matched set, but rather show off your differences, your femininity. As much as you might love the same team as your husband, wearing matching team jerseys is a slippery slope.

Travel. A little time and space creates the opportunity for yearning, renewed desire, and a romantic reunion.

Attend dinner parties and group get-togethers where your husband can enjoy your beauty and charm as reflected in another man's eyes. Resist the monetization of life. Make time to eat dinner together, at the table, with candles.

Finally, never, ever, ever pick up your dinner from a drive-
through. And I'm not saying this because it's probably not a
healthy choice, but rather, because I honestly don't think you're
going to meet the love of your life at the McDonald's window.
And you won't find your most radiant and joyful self reflected
there, either.

CHAPTER TWELVE

How to Heal a Broken Heart: Mimi's Story

Paris is always a good idea.
—AUDREY HEPBURN

YOU ARE THIRTY-FIVE YEARS OLD AND YOU have your whole life in front of you. You have a career in real estate, working with your father, and on weekends you go antiquing with your mother. You are the youngest of four daughters. Your mother is adorable—curvy and funny and madly in love with your charming father. Your father calls the two of you his Lucy and Ethel. He's a runner and slim and he loves the fact that his wife is curvy and girlish. Whenever she sees him, she will say in the most charming whisper, "Oh, here comes that handsome Walter."

You and your mother share a love for antiques. You shop the flea markets; you collect vintage dressing tables and French linens. You visit Paris and get to know all the markets. You are the auntie who takes your older sisters' children to Paris as a graduation gift. Ah, the Paris expert.

Oh, and you are in love with Nigel. You are already talking about long-term plans. He's in great shape. He's a runner and strong and healthy, just like your athletic father.

You are thirty-five. Your dad is sixty-seven. And then, without warning, your father dies.

And he is gone. Just like that. And in that moment, your world is reeling, and still the changes and the loss have just begun. Only you don't know that yet. You believe everything can go back to the way it was, and true, you and your mother are so very, very sad at losing her beloved Walter, your beloved father.

But you pick yourself up, brush yourself off, and keep going. You and Nigel get engaged. You buy the wedding dress, you plan the reception, and you purchase the invitations. Things are moving forward. Life renews itself. Things begin again.

And then Nigel dies. He is only forty-four years old. And he was a runner. But still, he has a brain aneurysm in his sleep and he is gone. And this is not the first time you've lost your love. You were engaged when you were twenty-four and your fiancé died tragically in a water-skiing accident. You say, "That's it for me. I've got my family and I've got my work. That's enough."

You are now thirty-eight years old. This world, you think— it is breaking you. You cannot take any more of this loss.

And then, one year later, your mother dies. She lost her Walter. She lost love. Of course, this is not what the doctors say. They say she died of a series of ministrokes, but you know the truth. She died of a broken heart.

It happened in 2005, and now you are thirty-nine years old. And it would seem that there is nothing left for you in this world, and so you do what generations of women have done before you—you pack your bags and you go to Paris. This is what Mimi did.

NOW VOYAGER

It's a brilliant day in early October and I am meeting Mimi Bleu, the creator of *Belle Inspiration Magazine*. Mimi launched the digital magazine (www.belleinspiration.com) in 2010—it's all about celebrating joie de vivre. At Café Bonaparte, we sit at the tiny café table facing the sidewalk, order our coffees, and begin our talk about life and love and Paris and women.

Mimi has a wonderful warmth and sweetness about her that is so comforting. She has beautiful hair and bright hazel eyes that twinkle a little when she laughs. And she does laugh, quite a lot. After everything that has happened to her, she certainly has not lost her sense of humor. She tells me her story of how her broken heart was healed.

"I had never come to Paris by myself before, but after everything that happened, I desperately needed a rest. It was May and so cold! I'm a Floridian, and I came dressed like a Floridian, so I had to buy all-new clothes."

Truthfully, this sounds kind of fun to me, but I don't say anything. She tells me that she stayed by the Champs-Elysées, near Ladurée—the famous patisserie where they make those magnificent macarons.

One evening, shortly after she arrived in Paris, she was strolling down the avenue when a man in a coat, carrying a briefcase, was coming from the opposite direction. As they walked closer and closer to each other and their eyes met and locked, she repeated over and over again to herself, *"Do not talk to anyone. I am not here to meet anyone!"*

Mimi takes a sip of her coffee and explains that this part of the Champs-Elysées is famous for pickups. Her eyes sparkle as she explains to me, *"You just stand there for two seconds and some dope says something to you."*

And so, once she passed the man, she slipped into a café and ordered a hot chocolate. She was cold and tired. The place was almost empty, so she sat at a corner table. She smoothed her skirt and picked up the menu and when she looked up again, there he was, walking in the door—the man from the street, the one with the coat and briefcase. This seemed very strange to her. After all, on the street, he was headed in the opposite direction.

"So I knew he must have backtracked, and I think, Oh no, I'm not up for this!"

But, apparently, he was up for this, because once the man spotted her, he planted himself at the table next to her. By this time, Mimi had ordered her hot chocolate (or *chocolat chaud*, as the French call it).

He didn't realize she was an American, and so he leaned over and said to her in French, *"I know where you can get an authentic hot chocolate."* She responded in English and then he quickly switched to English, and they talked and talked and talked. And talked. He told her his name is Jean-Pierre.

"I felt instantly at ease," Mimi confesses to me.

"But I was cautious. I was alone in Paris and on the plane over I had made up my mind to be careful because I just wasn't myself and wanted my parents to be proud of me. Still, I noticed his extremely dark eyes. That was the first thing to catch my attention. They were hard to resist! He also had this heart-melting smile to go with it and a nice, strong build."

He said, *"There's another café up the street, just three blocks up, and they have much better hot chocolate, and you'll be safe."* He explained how this particular part of the boulevard was a little bit tricky for beautiful women and he wanted to protect her from the local riffraff. But she refused his offer. And then he asked if she would join him for dinner. And again, she refused. He asked her if she'd like to get a drink with him, and she said no.

"I did ask myself, 'Why not?'" she tells me, *"But I was unhappy."* Mimi explained that after that she figured she'd never see him again. However, that's not what happened, because for the next few days, she would see him around the corner from her hotel, always at a different time. She bumped into him at random times on the Champs-Elysées. As it turns out, he was working nearby. During one of these encounters, he said to her, *"Just dinner?"* And she smiled and said, *"No, thanks."*

But after these almost-karmic encounters, she did begin to feel something. *"I actually kicked myself for the rest of the night for not accepting his offer."*

Finally, after running into Jean-Pierre for the third day in a row, she couldn't sleep, and she kept thinking about this mysterious French man.

SLEEPLESS IN THE CITY OF LIGHT

The next day, after a night of insomnia, she slept in and didn't leave the hotel until three in the afternoon. She bought a copy of the *Periscope*—the newspaper that lists current exhibitions and events—and she found a bench. Mimi sat and looked at the paper, and then she noticed a man's legs next to her. She looked up to find Jean-Pierre smiling at her. He said, *"Okay, I'm not following you. Clearly, this is meant to be."*

Once again, he invited her for a coffee. And this time, she said yes.

And nineteen months later, they married. Yes, of course, Mimi met Jean-Pierre's family and Jean-Pierre met Mimi's older sisters—who, as Mimi puts it, *"wanted to make sure little sister was thinking straight!"*

Mimi and Jean-Pierre have now been happily married for eleven years, and she has found a new life in Paris with the man who was always meant for her. He just happened to be French.

Oh, and what does Jean-Pierre say about Mimi? Well, this is what he tells me: *"When I saw her coming down the street, I thought, There she is—the one I've been waiting for. It was destiny."*

Mimi offers this advice on finding love: *"Be patient. But when the right time comes, it is always easy. When he's not right, it's not easy."*

Today, Mimi uses her expertise in the field of antiquing in Paris to offer private curated tours. She brings boutique owners from the United States and around the world, as well as individuals, couples, and lots of mother-and-daughter teams. She collects small sterling silver frames, and she loves "a good French desk," she says. *They are very feminine,* she tells me, and then adds, *"The key to antiquing is to practice restraint."* She smiles at me with the wisdom of a woman who has lived and lost love and loved again.

CHANGER LES IDÉES

Can you imagine what might have happened if Mimi had stayed at home, in Florida, bereft and broken-hearted? Well, she most assuredly would not have met the love of her life.

No, Mimi found love because she did what smart women do when they have hit a wall. They travel. They shake things up. They try something new. They *change les idées.* This expression doesn't simply mean to change your ideas or change your mind. It goes deeper and includes the idea of changing the way you think, changing your habits, your environment, and your worldview.

This change can be something big and dramatic, such as going to an ashram in India, or it can be something small, such as taking a pottery class. It can be joining Habitat for Humanity or something tiny such as changing how you wear your hair and painting your kitchen walls tangerine. Or chartreuse. Or aubergine. This tiny change begets another change and another change—and before you know it, you have pulled yourself out of that rut and created a new groove that has the potential to completely shake up your life.

You see, we get used to our routines. They feel familiar and safe. And when tragedy strikes, or when our hearts are smashed to pieces, we naturally want to retreat to what is safe and familiar. We want comfort. And as contradictory as this might sound, this is not the time to seek comfort, but to stretch and grow and challenge your own assumptions about who you are and the world you live in.

So, dear voyager, be brave and take flight. Your heart will thank you for it.

Parisian Charm School Lesson

Let go of the notion that there are money-back guarantees when it comes to love.

Think of your heart as a muscle. It must be stretched and used and broken and healed and then even broken again before it is strong and resilient.

The French do not think about "getting back in the game," but rather how they can comfort and console their wounded spirit. French women take their time with this healing process, and you can, too.

> KNOW THIS: WHEN THE TIME
> IS RIGHT, LOVE WILL RETURN,
> AND IT WILL FEEL EASY.

Cultivate your own secret garden; where can you find your personal wellspring? Still, it's important to get out of your comfort zone and take this opportunity to shake things up. Perhaps you need to book a trip to Paris. But then again, perhaps you need to return to your ancestral home in Puerto Rico or follow your intuitive voice that tells you that you must see the northern lights this summer in Iceland. Then again, if you're obsessed with Victoria and *Downton Abbey*, then go to England. Or perhaps you realize, as Dorothy did, "there's no place like home." Then return. But first, go someplace new and meet new friends. Open your heart.

Parisian Charm School Pratique

Your heart should have an emergency first aid kit at the ready, because while you may not have a broken heart at this moment, one day you will have a broken heart, so prepare.

Make a list of the things that bring you solace and that make you feel strong.

Ask yourself if there is a place you might go to find your courage once again. You don't have to go there right away, but you might put a photograph of this place in your emergency kit.

Finally, live your life with an open heart. Yes, it may get broken, but you will survive.

CHAPTER THIRTEEN

Histoires d'Amour

(Love Stories from French Women)

*Love is a canvas furnished by nature and
embroidered by imagination.*
—VOLTAIRE

FRENCH WOMEN OFTEN USE THE EXPRESSION "my love story." I don't think this idea of a "love story" is a translation issue, but rather, it's simply the way they think. Their love life is a story. It's artful and it's always evolving and changing.

If you think about love in this way, you see the long view. There is no "goal" of getting a boyfriend or getting married, but rather there is a beautiful story that's unique and perfect in its own way.

I've talked to many French women and men, and their stories of how they met are all very interesting. They meet in a variety of ways—a glance across the metro platform leads to a chance encounter the next day and then a rendezvous in the park. Many of my French women friends meet through introductions from other friends. I know several women who have met their boyfriends at workshops. Cooking classes seem to be a particularly fertile crowd for romance. My friend Isabelle met her husband at a family party. And Isaure met a wonderful man in the middle of a rainstorm in the Marais, where they were huddled together under an awning, getting soaking wet and laughing.

NON, JE NE REGRETTE RIEN!

Not too long ago, the photographer Krystal Kenney told me her love story. She's a beautiful girl with long auburn hair and blue-blue eyes. She really looks as if she walked out of a poster advertising the beautiful people of Ireland, but she's actually an American from suburban Maryland. She reminds me a little of my daughter, who's also a photographer (now a graphic designer). They're around the same age, and so I feel an immediate rapport with Krystal. She's been living in Paris for the past four years.

She arrived in Paris after graduating from university during the 2008 economic crisis in America.

> "With a boatload of student debt and no real job prospects in sight, it seemed like the perfect time to throw caution to the wind and take a vacation in Europe. Six countries later and no richer, I was back in America with what I like to call reverse culture shock. I quickly realized that out of all the countries I visited, France had my heart, and I had to find a way to get back and make my life there."

Krystal returned back home once more, full of new energy and ambition. She took five different jobs while running her own photography company, cleared out all her student debt, sold her car, moved to Paris, and became a full-time photographer.

Krystal has photographed some pretty famous people, such as the writers John Irving and Michael Chabon as well as the American ambassador to Paris and the singer Jimmy Buffett. I feel very fortunate to be in such stellar company!

Oh, and she's also brilliant at finding the secret and not-so-secret spots to stage our photo shoot.

This morning, we've been prancing around the Palais Royale, and Krystal has taken dozens of photos of me, posing in the gardens, switching hats and scarves, and turning from left to right, changing from close-up shots to me in the distance with an entire garden behind me.

And now we are relaxing with our café crème at Café Nemours.

Krystal tells me about her romantic life in Paris. She explains how it has opened her mind and heart to new adventures.

"When we carry on the same routines daily in an environment we are accustomed to, we miss so much. When you are constantly stimulated by trying to figure out a language, a new city, a new group of humans, our brain is fluttering with activity and jumps out of autopilot into reality and possibilities."

Oh, and the possibilities of finding new love!

"I met my boyfriend, Jacques, in a very strange way. I was on my way from photographing a gala. By the end of the night, I was en-joying some of the perks of photographing parties, which included a few glasses of free champagne. After a fun night of dancing and

meeting new people, I was feeling energized and happy as I made my way to the metro platform.

"As the train approached a handsome, tall brunette stepped up next to me. I felt a shock of energy run through my body as I watched him in my peripheral vision.

"I took care to sit across from him on the metro so I could look closer, but not too close. I kept staring at him in the reflection of the metro window.

"Every few stops his eyes would lock with mine in the reflection and we would both smile and look away.

"My stop arrived, and he got off first. And by coincidence this was my stop, too! I began to walk in the opposite direction up the stairs, but stopped one last time to look over my shoulder and smile at this handsome young man.

"And then he turned around at exactly the same moment. We locked eyes, and he turned around to approach me. 'Bonjour,' he said with a coy smile."

Krystal and Jacques lived happily together for over two years. And yes, there was quite a bit of drama here and there, but there was also some true romance for our young photographer. Jacques helped Krystal navigate French customs, administration, and the language. They traveled together throughout Europe and truthfully this was a fairy-tale story—the American and the quintessential French man. In the end, their love story came to an end, but Krystal is quite young and she is happy to be on her own once again with, perhaps, her true love—Paris.

LOVE ACROSS THE CONTINENTAL DIVIDE

Ondine is a clothing designer and style consultant. She's working on a memoir told through shoes, and that alone makes me adore her! Ondine is originally from the South of France, but I first met her in Boston, where she was designing clothes for performers and patrons of the arts. She received her clients at her atelier on Beacon Street, where she was (and still is) an image consultant. She's helped hundreds of women and men who felt fashionably challenged or just wanted to freshen up their look. Oh, and if that wasn't enough—she also works as a plus-size model.

LOVE IN PARIS

Ondine is a luscious and very feminine woman, with an engaging smile and lots of joie de vivre. She tells me that her signature fragrance is Shalimar, but she wears Yves Saint Laurent's Manifesto when she's feeling especially bold. She just makes you feel happy to be alive, and happy to be in Paris, sitting at the Café Roc with her, discussing life and style and fashion and perfume, and of course, love.

Here's what she told me about meeting the love of her life:

"It was a Saturday in November, and I was having the best hair day of my life.

"I had been to see Sebastien de Paris, who received clients at a posh salon on Avenue Franklin Roosevelt in the eighth arrondissement. I walked out of the salon feeling like the cutest girl in Paris. I was supposed to go on a date with a Russian count (Boris) that night, but he was called away to Stockholm, so I decided to join

my girlfriends at the pub for a birth-day celebration.

"I must have been exuding a very charming vibe with my new coupe *(haircut) because I was chatting with three guys at once when Jérôme walked in. I saw him immediately (he's tall) over the other guys' heads, and we made eye contact. I was struck by his big dark eyes and full eyebrows. He's classically handsome, almost in an old-fashioned way. Just picture Gregory Peck plus Sean Connery. And when he smiled, his whole face got involved, especially his eyes. Also, I loved his long arms and legs, his hands and broad shoulders.*

"Obviously, something happened. Was it love at first sight? I don't know. I only know that I had a feeling we had met before and that he was a sweet person.

"We were introduced by a mutual friend (who was drunk at the time and didn't remember the fateful incident at all). Jérôme asked me if I'd like to go out, but I was no longer living in Paris. I was only back for a fortnight and then I would return to Boston. Still, he wasn't dissuaded.

"We met for coffee the next day. I had dinner plans with friends, so I arranged to meet him a couple of hours before. We met at Metro Saint-Paul and walked to a nearby café, where we stared at each other, smiling, over espresso. He was wearing a gray sweater. The collar was stretched out, and I could see his neck and

his collarbone. I loved how this view of his neck was so beguiling and exciting—a hint of things to come, perhaps. It was sexy and yet discreet and natural.

"After coffee, we walked hand in hand to meet up with my friends. He kissed me good night and left. When he was out of earshot, my friends declared, 'Il est mignon!' ('He is darling!') and asked how long we'd been dating.

"Two hours.

"Later that night, during dinner with my friends in the Marais, Jérôme sent me a text. He didn't want to disturb me but he had to tell me that he was 'sur un petit nuage' (floating on a little cloud).

"After this, we went out every day for the next week (strolls in Le Jardin du Luxembourg, Île Saint-Louis, pizza on Rue des Canettes), and finally it was time for me to return to Boston. I had already fallen for him and was heartbroken that our story would be over.

"'I'll come to Boston,' he said.

"'Sure,' I sobbed, thinking I would never see him again.

"Three weeks later we were reunited at Logan Airport. He had never been to the States before. His English was . . . shaky.

"He later confided that he was terrified I wouldn't be there to meet him. We commuted between Paris and Boston for two years and eventually married each other in 2010 on three different continents. Our son, Logan Charles, was born the following year, and two years later, our daughter, Paloma. The name Charles is to honor my father, Charles, who passed away six weeks after we were married in his house in Thailand. People often ask us if Logan is named for the airports—Boston Logan and Paris Charles de Gaulle. After all, they were the hubs of our lives for many years, so that's a bonus significance!

*"This November will be the tenth anniversary of my very best
hair day ever!"*

LOVE FINDS YOU

Nicole, my Parisian friend with the beautiful voice—the one
who took me to La Mascotte for dinner in Paris—recently
joined me at French Roast in the West Village in New York
City. Oh, and she introduced me to her husband, Angel.

Angel is a soft-spoken fellow and doesn't speak much English, and so while Nicole and I chattered away, he quietly looked
on and listened and probably understood a lot more than he let
on, because his eyes were very bright and he smiled and nodded
and I thought, how lucky for Nicole to have such a sweet man
as her life partner. Nicole told me that they met as children.
They grew up in the same village in the southwest of France
and Nicole was friends with Angel's older sisters. They didn't
really go out in the same circles, because while Nicole was seventeen, Angel was only fourteen—a million years' difference in
teen years. And so she didn't really notice him.

However, Angel noticed Nicole. He leans forward and tells
me how he admired this "older woman." She is *très élégante.*
Differente. Very cool. Stylish. So, it would seem that even in high
school, Nicole was destined for a life in Parisian fashion and not
a life in the country. But Angel had such a big crush on her, he
simply never forgot about her.

Years went by and Nicole moved to Paris, and they lost track
of one another and went on with their lives. They didn't see each
other for over thirty years, until one day Angel's sisters phoned
Nicole from their home village to say that they'd love to get

together again, after all these years. And they mentioned that their younger brother had recently divorced. Nicole had never married. Still, she didn't understand why Angel's sister would want her to meet with her brother. She hadn't really known Angel in school, but then Angel invited her out to dinner, and so she accepted the invitation and arrangements were made.

A week later, Nicole returned to her family's village and she met Angel and they went to dinner at a nice restaurant. Nicole tells me that their village is very much like my favorite village, Auvillar—with its ancient buildings and artistic community. That night over dinner, Nicole learned that since she last saw Angel, when he was a young man, he'd become a martial art master and was the French champion for tae kwon do six years in a row and had traveled to Korea for competitions. So in the intervening years, Angel had grown into a very interesting and successful man.

And Nicole and Angel love to visit the States. They married on the beach in Cape Cod on June 1, 2014, thanks to their American friends.

Nicole and Angel have been together for fourteen years, but because of work they do not actually live together. Still, Nicole assures me that France has a very good network of airplanes and speed trains, so they easily meet in Paris or the South of France by the Mediterranean coast.

When I ask the couple if they would like to offer any advice to my American readers on how to find love, here's how they replied:

"We are very different. All those differences nourish our relationship. Our encounter, after all those years, was completely unexpected.

You have to stay open-minded and let life surprise you. Things happen when you least expect them to happen. Never give up. You don't find love when you're searching for it. Love finds you!"

OH, CANADA!

Ever since my first book, *French Women Don't Sleep Alone,* came out, people ask me about what happened to "the girl in the skirt and boots." That girl is my good friend Jessica Lee. She came with me to France in 2007 as my translator. She had just finished a really difficult year.

"I had managed to extract myself from a destructive and manipulative relationship that had nearly killed my spirit and had left me with no self-confidence; a close friend died of cancer, and I also lost my grandmother, to whom I was very close."

In this fragile state, Jessica began our trip wearing jeans and T-shirts and ended it by wearing skirts and boots and flirting like a French woman. But, more than this, it wasn't long before she found true love. Here's her beautiful love story in her own words:

"The trip to France changed my way of thinking. I listened to the women we met with great interest. They were romantic but pragmatic. Their relationships were also friendships, and had started as friendships, or quasi-friendships, or friend-of-a-friend friendships, whereas my relationships had always started out as individual encounters with strangers that became romantic.

"When I met Marc, I was just beginning my second year as a French teacher and was at a language conference, passing through

the exhibitors' floor, when I noticed a sign that read FRENCH! IN CANADA! *The table really had the worst possible placement: a desolate little corner. 'I'll come talk to you,' I said. He stood up. 'Please do.'*

"I remember that we talked about French immersion and Canadian health care. He remembers that we talked about anything and everything and that I made fun of him for having a PC. During that conversation, it suddenly dawned on me that he was very handsome . . . his broad smile, his brown eyes, framed in squarish blue glasses. He also spoke French and English perfectly, and he wasn't wearing a ring. Hmmm, I thought, and listened with increasing interest.

"The next morning, I drove back to the conference, made a beeline for the exhibitors' floor, and then pretended to wander around casually, as if I hadn't come just for him. I was on a tight schedule. I had a plan. 'Hey, you're Canadian,' I said. 'You don't know anyone here. And you speak French. I am going to a party tonight with a bunch of French people. You should come.' I handed him my card. A few hours later, I received a text accepting my invitation.

"At the party, he seemed to talk to everyone but me. 'He's off my list,' I told my friend Isaure, making a scratching motion.

"However after that, the notes started arriving. Within a month, we were talking on the phone, and another month later, I went to see him in Canada.

"That first night, we went to dinner and talked and talked and talked. The waiter came with the food, and it just sat on the plates. Time streamed by and then they closed the restaurant. I remember a still-full plate being taken away. I didn't even feel hungry. The weekend continued that way. Conversation flowed easily and fluidly, unlike the other dates I had had throughout my lifetime, *where it felt like a bad tennis match, or worse, an inquisition, searching for something to ask in order to find some common ground. With him, I didn't have to think about what I was saying. There seemed to be endless topics to cover.*

"I went home feeling great, but also hesitant. He was extremely inconvenient: divorced with two young kids, and rooted in a different country that was an eight-hour drive or a plane ride away. I tried not to think about him. I even tried to meet other people in my own country, but Canada, as I called him, was just too interesting, too nice, too smart, too funny, too present. He was always on my mind. And then I finally gave in to chance. I had decided that I needed to risk in order to love, and if love included the possibility of hurt, so be it.

"We started a long-distance romance, flying back and forth once or twice a month for nearly three years. When he asked me to come to Canada, it was a huge decision: leave my country, my family, my friends, everything I knew. But I loved him. It seemed like I had waited my entire life to meet him. Being with Marc made me realize that I had never really been myself with anyone else. With him, it was easy; it wasn't like pushing a boulder uphill.

"My father had always told me, 'Just do what you do and eventually you will probably notice the right person doing it right alongside you.' He was right."

SAY YES—TO THE UNKNOWN,
TO THE POSSIBILITY OF
GETTING HURT. JUST SAY YES.

Today, Jessica and Marc are married and live with his two remarkable boys. Jessica is an editor, a French teacher, and a brilliant translator.

SAY YES

As it turns out, the day I brought the big pink lilies to my French friend Sylvie would be the last time I saw her, the girl who started it all. I don't tell you this to make you sad, but just to remind you that our time in this world is limited and to suggest that when you see those flowers and a group of French ladies laughing and gesturing for you to join them and pick out some flowers, you should say yes.

Just say yes, even though it might seem strange and you're not exactly sure what these French ladies are saying to you.

Just say yes, even though you've already bought a box of chocolates and this would be just one more thing to carry through the streets of Paris.

Just say yes, even though you don't have wrapping paper or a ribbon for those flowers.

Just say yes, even though there's the danger of getting yellow pollen smudged on your pretty white American blouse. In fact, that's especially when you say yes to the flowers, to the world, to your friends, to your man, to life. Know this: there will be times in your life when you are offered something lovely, but there will be pollen and there will be the certain danger that you will find yourself forever marked, forever changed.

Still, say yes.

Parisian Charm School Lesson

You are living your own true, unique love story. Love yourself. Love the people around you and love life. Embrace the idea

Be open to the possibility of the unexpected surprise. that you have all the time in the world because your love story will unfold in its own special way.

Consider the circuitous path to finding the love of your life as part of the delicious journey. Take a step back from goal-oriented dating and think of your love life in the long view. Relax, knowing that love is whimsical and unpredictable.

Be open to the possibility of the unexpected surprise. And create your own beautiful love story. And finally, throw out the idea of perfection.

Parisian Charm School Pratique

Very simple. Trust your heart. Say yes. And bring the flowers.

Parisian Charm School
Glossary

Absolument! Absolutely. Definitely. *Yes. Of course.*

À la française. The French way.

Amour. Love, in English and French.

Apéro. A drink before dinner, short for "aperitif."

Armagnac. A beloved and delicious brandy from the southwest of France, often enjoyed at the end of a good meal.

Arrondissement. Neighborhood.

Ballerinas—Ballerinas. Refers to any kind of ballerina-inspired flats. They can have rounded toes or be pointy. They can be flat or have little heels. They're a must-have in any French woman's wardrobe, particularly from Repetto, where they come in a crayon box full of colors.

BiBaCa. Short for *Biclou Baguette & Camembert.* A bicycle, a baguette, and some camembert.

Bisous. A kiss on each cheek. A typical French greeting.

Boulangerie. A bakery, distinguished from *patisserie*, which sells pastries and desserts; the *boulangerie* specializes in breads.

Cage d'amour. Literally, cage of love. An orange flower that looks like a Chinese lantern.

Chambre Bleue. The Blue Room. An intellectual salon created by Catherine de Vivonne, the Marquise de Rambouillet, in the seventeenth century.

Chambre de bonne. This small room, located on the top floor, was traditionally the bedroom for servants, with a separate entrance. Equivalent to a small studio apartment.

Changez d'itineraire. Change your itinerary, change your horizons.

Changer les idées. Change your ideas, your point of view, and ultimately, your life.

Chinoiserie. Decorative elements inspired by Asia, mostly from the 1800s. Very popular with certain French women.

Conter fleurette. To talk like a flower, sweet talk.

Coup de foudre. Literally, a strike of lightning, but often used to describe love at first sight.

Cresson. Watercress. A very popular vegetable in France, given to honor marathon runners in certain French villages.

Daube. Similar to our beef stew, except it's made with red wine.

De trop. Too much. A bigger sin than you might imagine, in France.

Fromage. Cheese. Very important in France, where there are at least four hundred different types.

Gastronomique. Enjoying really good food. An important pastime in France.

Gâteau au yaourt. Yogurt cake. The French make this simple cake using their yogurt cups for measurement.

Haute couture. High fashion, tailored, as opposed to ready-to-wear.

Hôtel Particulier. An historic, freestanding private mansion. Also, the name of a hotel and restaurant in Montmartre.

Je m'aime! I love myself.

Je ne regrette de rien. I regret nothing! Made famous by the French singer Édith Piaf.

Joie de vivre. Literally, joy of life. A French expression that encompasses the idea of appreciating all the simple pleasures of life.

La ponctualité est la politesse des rois. Punctuality is the politeness of kings. In other words, charming women show up on time.

La Rentrée. The return to school or work. The energetic period after a six-week (sometimes four-week) summer holiday, where the French return home, renewed, refreshed, and ready for the new season's exhibitions and cultural offerings.

Le Bleuet de France. Literally, the blue of France. Refers to the French uniforms during World War I.

Le Jardin d'Iseult. The garden of Iseult named after the 12th-century Anglo-Norman literature, inspired by the Celtic legend.

Le Jardin du Port. The Garden of the Port.

Le regard. The look a man will give you when he notices you. French women take care to look their best when they go out so that they might encourage being noticed by both men and women.

Le Rock. Partner dancing, like in the 1950s, including twirling.

Les Perle des Dieux. Pearls of the sea. A brand of very delicious and special sardines that can be purchased at the iconic Montmartre seafood brasserie La Mascotte.

Madame Gentille. Madame Sweet.

Mariner. The striped Breton shirt made famous by Coco Chanel and Bridget Bardot. A staple in every French woman's wardrobe. Petit Bateau is a famous and beloved creator of an array of mariners.

Mettre son grain de sel. To add my grain of salt, or my two cents' worth.

Mon dieu. My God! or My goodness!

N'est ce-pas? Is it not?

Objet d'art. An object of art. Anything can be an artful object when considered with the French eye for beauty and elegance.

Oh la la! A French expression related to *de trop*, as in "too much!" It's used to convey some sort of distress.

Ooh la la! An Americanization of the French *Oh la la!* and as we know, means something is fabulous or sexy. It can be traced to 1920s, when Americans flocked to Paris during the wild and wonderful jazz age and when *de trop* (too much) became just enough.

Orezza. A brand of sparkling water with "delicate bubbles." The French talk about "brutal bubbles" found in some other sparkling waters and are very particular about where their sparkling waters come from. (See *terroir.*)

Paris plages. Paris beaches. In 2006, the mayor of Paris closed off the roads along the Seine River and created artificial beaches so that Parisians could enjoy the feeling of being at a seaside resort without actually leaving town.

Robe des champs. Literally the dress that you wear in the fields, but in cooking when it comes to potatoes it means with the skins still on.

Salon du vintage. The vintage market. Refers to the annual Paris event featuring vintage clothing, housewares, jewelry, records, and much, much more.

Saucisson. Salami. Typical picnic fare.

Secret de Jardin en Essonne. The Secret Garden in Essonne, a small town west of Paris. During the fall, there are secret garden parties throughout France, celebrating the lush gifts of nature.

Spécialité de la maison. The speciality of the house.

Sur un petit nuage. On a little cloud, as in "floating" on a little cloud. Equivalent to our "floating on air."

Terroir. Literally, "land," but the concept encompasses all the elements that make up the character of land, including the climate and the geological makeup of the soil. Generally used to describe the origin of a particular wine.

Titi Parisienne. Typically Parisienne.

Un flâneur. A person who strolls. The French embrace this concept with open arms and great enthusiasm.

Une femme d'un certain âge. A woman of a certain age.

Vélib'. Rental bike. A very important mode of transportation, especially in Paris where women will ride the bikes wearing heels and pretty dresses.

Ville de Lumière. City of Light, aka Paris.

Vive la différence. "Long live difference," often used to refer to the difference between men and women. The secret to French amour.

Acknowledgments

*It's as difficult to make a good jam
as it is to make a good book.*
—GEORGE SAND

CONGRATULATIONS, DEAR READER, YOU'VE
arrived at the end of your *Parisian Charm School* journey and it's
now time for me to bid you farewell.

If you were actually enrolled in a Parisian Charm School, we
would hold a big graduation ceremony with caps and gowns
and hugs and tears and an inspiring commencement speech.

This would be the part where the head schoolmistress (that
would be *moi*) would step up to the podium and thank the students, the teachers, the administration, the friends, and all the
wonderful individuals who made all this possible. And with that
in mind, I begin my thanks.

I am so very, very grateful to my wonderful agent, Irene
Goodman, who worked tirelessly with me to create a proposal,
a title, and the concept for *Parisian Charm School.*

I am also thrilled to thank my new editor at Penguin Random House, Marian Lizzi. She has been a dedicated expert and trusted advisor to *Parisian Charm School*, guiding me through a most enjoyable process. I am also so grateful to Lauren Appleton, Associate Editor, and Janet Robbins Rosenberg, my copy editor extraordinaire.

My deep gratitude goes out to my beautiful friend and traveling companion Jessica Lee. Jessica has always stood by my side, reading and editing my pages, checking my French, my grammar, my spelling. In fact, I consider her the unofficial director of the French language department of *Parisian Charm School*.

I would also like to thank my brilliant readers Marianne Schmidt, Kelly Kynion, and Lindsay Ahl. They are all both smart and sweet.

I send out a big *merci beaucoup* to all my dear friends living in France, who generously offered their insights, quotes, recipes, and love stories: Edith de Belleville, Aloïs Guinut, Freddie Duvignacq, Pierre Dubernet, Kate Kemp-Griffin, Christian Kemp-Griffin, Mimi Bleu, Valerie Bloch, Krystal Kenney, Rhonda Richford, Nicole Bergeaud, Angel, Edith and Marcelle, Renata Dancale, Marine Bordos, Denise Siméon, Jim Haynes, Havoise Mignotte, Ondine Brent Eysseric, Micheline Tanguy, Carol Gillot, and Nancy Flavin.

I would also like to send a shout out to my friends and family who offered their thoughts on dance, flowers, love, cooking and more: Amy Couch, Anne Marie Mink, Marc Gobiel, Heather Johnson, Beverly Aker, Alexandra Bader, Denise Chranowski, Susan Gubernat, Karen Malina, my very supportive dad, and my dear daughter, Callan Silver.

I offer a big heartfelt appreciation to my beautiful and very wise French teacher, Madame M., for always being by my side and offering me her gracious love, wisdom, and support.

I thank the Virginia Center for the Creative Arts for an international fellowship to write in Auvillar, France. I thank Cheryl and John for the good company and the friendship during my residency.

I am forever grateful to my husband, Dr. Thompson, who gave me the gift of my own private artists' colony here at our home on La Belle Farm so that I could completely devote myself to writing this book.

And finally, I want to thank you, sweet reader, for all your inspiration and support over these many years.

Please know this: charm is free and it's available to everyone. And here's the magical part: the more you practice the art of charm, the more charming the world around you becomes.

Now I release you from *Parisian Charm School,* I wish you all the goodness and grace this life has to offer.

Now go and be charming.

Index

in America, 7–8
French attitudes toward,
138–39, 179
online dating, 7, 26
See also love and romance
daube recipe of Dubernet, 131,
132–33
differences, embracing, 187
dignity, 155
dinner parties, 123–41
and attractiveness in marriage,
165, 166–67
beef bourguignon recipe for, 131,
132–33
and Biclou Baguette &
Camembert event, 127–28
cake recipe for, 136, 137
casual, 127, 140
developing charm in, 140
and essentials for the kitchen,
129–30
hosting, 140–41
Jim Haynes's soirées, 124–26
paella recipe for, 134, 135–36
and romance, 138–40
and value of waiting in line,
126–27
dress codes, 88–89
Dress Like a Parisian blog, 23
Duvelleroy, 103–6

eating alone, 154
Edith's Paris tours, 12
education, 15, 102–3
Eiffel Tower, 49, 114
emotions
prompted by articles of clothing,
32, 34, 35
and reactions to colors, 90, 93
Epictetus, 23
excess, eliminating, 151

existentialism of the French, 144
experiential pleasures,
emphasizing, 159

familiarity, 155, 157
family
and birthright, 35
and flirtation of previous
generations, 108–9
honoring history of, 30–31, 36
old photographs of, 35
and personal style, 29–32,
33, 35
and reactions to colors, 90
fans, hand, 17, 103–6
Fauchon, 85
flirtation, 95–109
accessories used in, 103–6, 109
alone with a man, 97
in America, 95
Belleville on, 16
and color choices, 93
and commerce in America, 163
and dinner parties, 140
with eyes only, 108
and fans, 103–6
and flowers, 73–75
and formality, 99
and French salons, 102–3
and group activities, 97
importance of, 96
and intimacy, 99–100
of Madame M., 97–98
and principles of seduction, 99
and private moments in public
spaces, 101–2, 108
purpose of, 96
and romance in marriage,
162–63, 165
for shy people, 103–6, 107
trifecta of, 74–75

ABOUT THE AUTHOR

Jamie Cat Callan is the author of the best-selling books *French Women Don't Sleep Alone; Bonjour, Happiness!;* and *Ooh La La! French Women's Secrets to Feeling Beautiful Every Day.* Her books have been published in twenty-two countries: the United States, Germany, Italy, Brazil, Japan, Taiwan, the Czech Republic, the Philippines, Poland, Russia, China, Romania, Portugal, Croatia, Lithuania, Korea, Serbia, Turkey, Ukraine, Canada, Australia, and New Zealand.

Jamie's books have been featured in major publications, including the *New York Times, Cosmopolitan, Allure, Glamour, Elle, Vanity Fair,* and *Time* magazine.

Jamie has spoken to thousands of women (and more than a few men) encouraging them to embrace a life of romance, beauty, and style. Jamie has appeared on the international television news program *France 24,* as well as Plum TV and Better TV. Her work has inspired a new generation of women to discover their unique style and for women of a certain age to reclaim their joie de vivre.

Jamie makes her home in New York's Hudson Valley at La Belle Farm, where she and her husband have created a little bit of France and grow lavender and sunflowers and produce their own brand of French-inspired sparkling apple cider.

Learn more about Jamie at www.JamieCatCallan.com, and follow Jamie on Facebook, Instagram, and Twitter.